FOREWORD

I will remember 2010 as one of the most eventful years in the history of the European Union.

The year was dominated by the sovereign debt crisis affecting the euro area. At times, it was difficult to see what would happen next. At times, we were stretched to our limits. At times, we had to take exceptional measures. That we weathered the storm is a testament to the determination and solidarity that exists in the European Union.

The sovereign debt crisis has shown that we are more interdependent than ever before. A problem in one country can quickly become a problem for everyone. And the response of one government has a direct bearing on the options for other governments, whether in or outside the euro area. That is why we have reacted with a strong determination to deliver fiscal consolidation, not as an end in itself, but as a means of securing our future growth, jobs and prosperity. We are learning from the mistakes of the past by introducing decisions that alter the way we all behave in the future.

In 2010, we approved the financial programmes for Greece and Ireland and guaranteed the stability of the euro. The agreement on a safety net of €750 billion in May and the commitment to a permanent crisis fund from 2013 were the crucial steps to provide the stability needed.

It has led to the commitment from all 27 Member States that we must not find ourselves in this situation again. That is why the Commission has presented legislative proposals for a new economic governance approach. I hope that our monetary union will soon be complemented with the long overdue economic union.

We have also brought effective supervision and regulation to our financial markets. One year ago, few would have believed that we would have a new system of supervision for our financial markets in place from 1 January 2011. I strongly believe this is one of the best examples of how Europe can show it is delivering change.

As we look forward to the year ahead, it is clear that 2011 will define the sort of Europe that emerges in the future.

Building the economic recovery will be just as important in the next 12 months. Fiscal consolidation, structural reforms and growth-related reforms must be the priority.

A central part of our new approach will be the new European semester, which combines tighter fiscal rules, by reinforcing the Stability and Growth Pact, with effective economic coordination. This, together with adoption of the Commission's proposals on economic governance, before the summer, will be a quantum leap in terms of how we deal with economic issues in Europe.

From energy to innovation, from the digital agenda to education, from industry to the environment, we need to stimulate growth in Europe's new economy. We cannot go back to the imbalances that existed before the crisis. Only through new forms of growth will we see a return of confidence and the creation of new jobs. The Commission will make proposals in every one of these areas so that we have a medium-term strategy to back up our short-term crisis management.

GENERAL REPORT
ON THE ACTIVITIES
OF THE EUROPEAN UNION
2010

WITHDRAWN

CONTENTS

During the last 12 months, we have kicked off the debate on how Europe can best invest its resources. I want to see the European Union concentrate on action that helps our economies grow and stimulates jobs. We need to invest our money where we get most value for it. And we should invest it where it leverages growth and delivers on our European agenda. The quality of expenditure should be the yardstick for us all.

My approach is that the European Union must provide value added and deliver real benefits to its citizens. We need to increase the benefits for citizens and businesses that are brought from the single market. We need to protect consumers better and make sure that companies are able to compete fairly across borders.

Europe must also have a single market of citizens' rights and values. A fundamental dimension of our Europe is building an area of freedom, security and justice. We are working hard to implement the Stockholm action plan. We will make a real push on asylum and legal and illegal migration.

How Europe can better project itself politically and economically in the world has never been more important. As the strategic partnerships of the 21st century emerge, Europe should seize the chance to define its future. I am impatient to see the Union play the role in global affairs that matches its economic weight. Our partners are watching and are expecting us to engage as Europe, not just as 27 individual countries. The establishment of the European External Action Service is a major step forward in bringing coherence to our external action. From the G20 to the development agenda for the millennium development goals, I am proud to say the Commission is now contributing to a much more assertive role of the European Union.

The year 2010 has been about delivering policies that make a difference to our citizens. To achieve that, we have introduced important changes to the way our institutions work. I have had the privilege to lead a new team of Commissioners. It has been a tough first year, but I'm proud of the central role that the Commission has played in steering the European Union through the economic crisis and designing the policy response. The Commission's proposals have set the agenda and provided the basis for the European Council to take the main strategic decisions. The European Council has now become an institution in its own right with a permanent President. This is a welcome development that provides stability and consistency to the representation of the 27 Member States. With a reinvigorated European Parliament that has new responsibilities, we have the stable institutional framework for the next few years that is essential if the European Union is to emerge stronger from this crisis.

The 2010 General Report gives a detailed overview of the activities of the European Union over the last year. I hope it stimulates more debate on the work that we do.

José Manuel Barroso

CHAPTER 1
DRIVING TOWARDS RECOVERY

The challenges that emerged to the EU's economic stability throughout the year were addressed with determination by the EU institutions.

The EU resolutely tackled the immediate threats to the public finances of Greece and Ireland, and to the stability of the euro.

In order to respond to the many challenges arising throughout the year the EU acted quickly and decisively to enhance short-term stabilisation. It then embarked on a far-reaching exercise of medium-term fiscal consolidation and reform of budgetary and economic surveillance.

The rapid design and implementation of first an emergency loan facility to Greece and then additional temporary financial support mechanisms for the euro area as a whole allowed Greece to begin repairing its domestic finances. Later in the year, the same prompt response made it possible to contain the risks posed by Ireland's acute economic difficulties. Steps were taken to provide a permanent European Stability Mechanism to come into effect as from 2013.

In parallel, new controls were introduced for the financial system, designed to prevent the recurrence of the problems that provoked the crisis of the last two years. Meanwhile, the EU worked with international partners to seek common action on issues in global economic governance that can reinforce growth and stability, promote trade and ensure a level playing-field.

EU leaders agreed at the June European Council on the European Commission's proposal for a 10-year programme for switching to high, sustainable growth. This Europe 2020 strategy ([1]), based on the political guidelines that President Barroso outlined for the new Commission in late 2009, will maximise the EU's assets, in particular the single market, and equip it for success in a rapidly changing world. It envisages full engagement of the Member States and identifies specific areas of action to turn ambition into achievement.

Linked to the Europe 2020 strategy, the EU approach to trade, enterprise, competition and the single market is being fine-tuned and updated. The full range of policies — from employment to environment, from citizens' rights to cohesion — are being refocused to ensure that the benefits are felt right across the EU.

ECONOMIC RECOVERY AND STRENGTHENED GOVERNANCE

As the events of the year so graphically demonstrated, what happens in one Member State may affect all the others. Restoring the EU as a whole to economic equilibrium meant supporting the Member States most in need. The EU's principle of solidarity took a very tangible form as joint action brought stability to national finances through providing access to credit. In response to the challenges faced by Greece, and to safeguard financial stability in the euro area as a whole, the EU rapidly set up temporary mechanisms to supply necessary lending, combined with strict policy conditions to put economies back on a sound footing. It thus bolstered confidence in euro-area public finances and in the credibility of the currency. It also promoted responsibility, particularly among the Member States concerned by mounting debt, which took their own vigorous action to consolidate public finances.

'The European Commission's top priorities right now — economic governance, the single market, innovation, industrial policy, jobs.'
José Manuel Barroso, 14 October

The events — and the proposed solutions — also generated an increased consensus among Member States and EU institutions. It became evident that assuring the future for the EU and its citizens depended on Member States getting a firmer grasp on the way that they run their national economies. As a result, the EU took steps to strengthen and modernise economic governance within the euro area and the wider EU by boosting coordination of fiscal and structural policies and reforms, including new attention to monitoring competitiveness. A task force chaired by Herman Van Rompuy, President of the European Council, made a number of recommendations calling for stricter adherence to the rules of the Stability and Growth Pact and fiscal prudence. The EU also acted to tighten up the rules governing the EU's economic and monetary union, including through enhanced surveillance of national budget plans, and a strengthening of sanctions against Member States that pursue irresponsible fiscal policies.

© European Union

German Chancellor Angela Merkel (right) and French President Nicolas Sarkozy (left) accompany Georgios Papandreou, Prime Minister of Greece, which was the first Member State to benefit from EU assistance.

SUPPORTING MEMBER STATES IN NEED

The EU took measures to secure financial stability, first through conditional financial assistance to Greece and then through the mechanisms for the euro area and the EU as a whole. In May, specific access to temporary financing was provided for Greece, which was unable to raise money on financial markets at affordable rates because of investors' fears that the country might default. The deal([2]), in which Member States (together with the International Monetary Fund (IMF) and the European Central Bank (ECB)) made available €110 billion, was based on strict conditions, a comprehensive and ambitious programme of structural reforms, and continuous monitoring. The package protects Greece from the need to raise money on the markets for up to two years, after which it is expected to return to market financing.

The EU moved with great speed, delivering financial support in the form of a guarantee within 10 days of the request. The rapid provision of this assistance was all the more remarkable in view of the fact that the EU treaties did not provide explicitly for instruments to deal with such an extraordinary situation. Euro-area leaders had to establish a financial rescue mechanism on the spot that fully respected both EU and Member State law. The Commission played a prominent role in the conception and adoption of the package, pooled the bilateral contributions into one common loan and negotiated the conditions with the Greek authorities.

'Our determination is clear. The Heads of State or Government of the euro area stand ready to do whatever is required to ensure the stability of the euro area as a whole.' Herman Van Rompuy, Brussels, 16 December

HOW THE EU HELPED GREECE AND IRELAND

In May, €110 billion was made available to Greece by the EU and the IMF.

In December, €85 billion was made available to Ireland by the EU, euro-area Member States, the United Kingdom, Sweden and Denmark, the IMF and the Irish Treasury and national pension reserve funds.

© AP / Reporters

Concerted EU action made it possible to contain the risks posed by acute economic difficulties in Ireland, where austerity measures provoked widespread public protest.

Then, in response to wider concerns about contagion in the euro area, a further and even more ambitious common effort by all EU institutions and Member States created — during the weekend of 7 to 9 May — two temporary support mechanisms for Member States. A total of €500 billion was made available, consisting of a €60 billion stabilisation mechanism for all Member States, administered by the Commission — the European Financial Stabilisation Mechanism (EFSM) — and an intergovernmental facility of €440 billion for euro-area Member States — the European Financial Stability Facility (EFSF) — administered by a specially created vehicle([3]). A further €250 billion from the IMF supplemented the sum. This unprecedented three-year stabilisation programme, with access subject to strict conditions, guarantees highly effective temporary support to euro-area countries experiencing soaring bond yields.

THE DETAILS OF THE NEW TEMPORARY MECHANISMS

The European Financial Stabilisation Mechanism (EFSM) consists of a maximum of €60 billion and is run by the European Commission, making use of the EU budget to raise money on the financial markets and on-lend the proceeds to a beneficiary Member State. The European Financial Stability Facility (EFSF) can provide up to €440 billion to help any euro-area country at risk of defaulting on its public debt. It is a special-purpose vehicle that will issue its own debt in order to provide loans in the event that a euro-area country is faced with serious financial difficulties. The facility's debt will be guaranteed by members of the euro area, as well as by Sweden and Poland, which volunteered to take part.

In late November, the Irish government requested financial assistance as the country ran into new difficulties in financing its borrowing. After intensive coordination, the Council, the Commission and the ECB agreed that providing assistance to Ireland was warranted to safeguard financial stability in the EU and in the euro area. They offered support under the EFSM and EFSF — the first time the new scheme was used. Finance ministers formalised the loan and the conditions attached to it in early December ([4]). The loans will be provided on the basis of a programme negotiated with the Irish authorities by the European Commission and the IMF, in liaison with the ECB. The three-pillar programme foresees: an overhaul of the Irish banking system; restoration of fiscal sustainability, including correction of the country's excessive deficit by 2015; and structural reforms to enhance growth. European assistance (including bilateral loans) amounts to €45 billion of the €85 billion package.

The ECB maintained its key policy interest rates at historically low levels throughout the year, alongside some non-standard measures to ensure an efficient transmission of the very low interest rates to the economy and, ultimately, to prices. A securities market programme enabled it to purchase euro-area public and private bonds, and to ensure depth and liquidity in dysfunctional segments in the government bond market so as to restore the proper functioning of the monetary policy transmission mechanism.

INFLATION AND INTEREST RATES

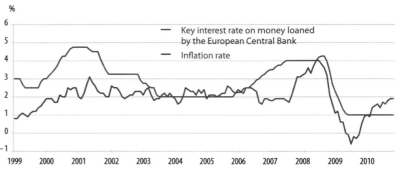

Key interest rate on money loaned by the European Central Bank

Inflation rate

Sources: European Commission/ECB.

ECB President Jean-Claude Trichet repeatedly stressed the ability of the euro to surmount the turbulence and pursued a policy of keeping interest rates at historically low levels.

At the same time, several countries started to implement consolidation measures to reduce budget deficits and restore fiscal sustainability within the common framework provided by the EU's Stability and Growth Pact. The solidarity that the EU expresses with Member States must be matched by their exercise of responsibility. The strict conditionality written into the stabilisation mechanisms created during the year presupposes that beneficiary states play their role fully in containing public spending and introducing reforms that will bring their finances back into balance.

The October European Council agreed that Member States should establish a permanent mechanism for crisis resolution to safeguard the financial stability of the euro area as a whole. The President of the European Council consulted with the members of the European Council on a limited treaty change. The result was agreement at the December European Council that the treaty should be amended to allow for the creation of the European Stability Mechanism (ESM). The aim is for the ESM to replace the EFSF and the EFSM in 2013. It will be activated by mutual agreement of the euro-area Member States in situations where the stability of the euro area as a whole is at risk.

THE PROPOSED TREATY CHANGE

The following paragraph shall be added to Article 136 of the Treaty on the Functioning of the European Union: '3. The Member States whose currency is the euro may establish a stability mechanism to be activated if indispensable to safeguard the stability of the euro area as a whole. The granting of any required financial assistance under the mechanism will be made subject to strict conditionality.'

GROWTH AND CRISIS

Growth in GDP, real annual change (%)
2011–12 are forecasts

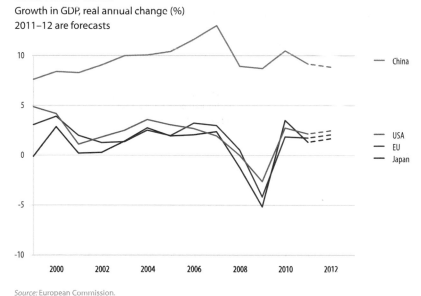

Source: European Commission.

THE EURO — A SOUND VALUE AMID TURBULENCE

The fundamentals of the euro are strong. It brings low inflation, a balanced current account, and underpins respectable economic growth — and it is the currency of reserve for large parts of the world. The euro withstood the pressures that it came under during the year, despite some volatility in its exchange rate. There was no crisis of the euro. The difficulties arose from individual Member States in the euro area that did not keep their public finances in order or improve their competitiveness.

STRENGTHENED ECONOMIC GOVERNANCE

The crisis revealed a lack of respect for rules on budgetary discipline, and inability to ensure that Member States follow sound economic policies oriented towards competitiveness. Over the course of the year, the Parliament, Council and Commission worked together on the construction of a new architecture to remedy these damaging deficiencies. They agreed on the principle of creating:

▶ a stronger surveillance regime, stricter and broader, covering budgetary, macroeconomic and structural policies and competitiveness gaps. The regime will reflect the interdependence that is central to the European economy. A scoreboard of indicators is envisaged to ensure early identification of large and increasing divergences, which will trigger recommendations for corrective action — backed by effective enforcement mechanisms. The new arrangements will promote the structural reforms, innovation and trade that can put Europe back on track in terms of sustainable and balanced growth, and create the jobs for the future.

Estonia joins the euro

The continued appeal of the euro was demonstrated when Estonia won the right to become a member of the euro area. Its request to join the single currency was accepted by the EU in June in order for it to become the 17th member of the club in January 2011. Estonia has a healthy economy and thereby fulfils the criteria for euro-area membership. It has managed to keep inflation and interest rates low. The country recorded a budget deficit of 1.7 % of GDP last year, well below the EU's 3 % limit. Government debt was also low — just 7.2 % of GDP. The economy is highly flexible and, while not immune to the crisis, has shown its ability to operate and adjust under a fixed exchange rate for close to two decades.

© Xinhua / Belga

Estonian Finance Minister Jürgen Ligi holds a symbolic euro coin during a ceremony in Brussels.

▶ a peer review of draft national budgets — known as the European semester, since it will take place in the first half of every year. As from 2011, Member States will present their stability and convergence programmes to the Commission in order to verify that they conform to the rules of the Stability and Growth Pact. To assure the quality of the necessary data, new powers have been agreed to allow verification of Member States' statistics. The review will also take account of plans to boost competitiveness and introduce necessary structural reforms. The result will be an enhancement of economic transparency and a more joined-up approach to budgeting, which will also be an asset for Member States as they plan, discuss and adopt their national budgets. In practice, the European semester will align the processes under the Stability and Growth Pact and the broad economic policy guidelines. It will cover fiscal discipline, macroeconomic stability and policies to foster growth in line with the Europe 2020 strategy.

▶ a reinforcement of the key rules of economic and monetary union — notably tightening up the Stability and Growth Pact, placing new emphasis on prudent fiscal policy-making in the medium-term, and a stronger focus on keeping debt under control. Sanctions are envisaged for Member States with fiscal policies that are not consistent with the European dimension. The European Parliament too called for priority to debt surveillance in a May resolution on the long-term sustainability of public finances.

Legislating for better economic governance

In September the Commission delivered a comprehensive package of legislative measures to reinforce economic governance in the EU and the euro area. It aims at broader and enhanced surveillance of fiscal policies, as well as of macroeconomic policies and structural reforms. It also provides new enforcement mechanisms for non-compliant Member States.

Four of the six proposals deal with fiscal issues, including a wide-ranging reform of the Stability and Growth Pact, so that sanctions will be the normal consequence for countries in breach of their commitments. Two other regulations aim at detecting and addressing emerging macroeconomic imbalances within the EU and the euro area.

- A regulation reinforcing the preventive role of the Stability and Growth Pact [5], to ensure that Member States follow prudent fiscal policies in good times to build up the necessary savings for bad times. Monitoring of public finances will be based on prudent fiscal policy-making, and the Commission can issue a warning in case of significant deviations.

- A regulation boosting the corrective role of the Pact [6] so that debt developments will be followed more closely, and the excessive deficit procedure can be invoked in the case of deviations. Member States whose debt exceeds 60 % of GDP should take steps to reduce it at a satisfactory pace. The regulation defines a debt-to-GDP ratio above 60 % as sufficiently diminishing if its distance with respect to the 60 % has reduced over the previous three years at a rate of the order of 1/20th per year. An excessive deficit procedure can be opened in the case of deviations.

- A regulation on effective enforcement of budgetary surveillance in the euro area [7], backing up the changes in the Pact with a new set of gradual financial sanctions for euro-area Member States. In preventive measures, an interest-bearing deposit should be the consequence of significant deviations from prudent fiscal policy-making. In the corrective part, a non-interest-bearing deposit amounting to 0.2 % of GDP would apply upon a decision to place a country in excessive deficit. This would be converted into a fine in the event of non-compliance with the recommendation to correct the excessive deficit. To ensure enforcement, a 'reverse voting mechanism' will be employed for imposing sanctions: this means that the Commission's proposal for a sanction will be considered adopted unless the Council turns it down by qualified majority.

- A directive on requirements for the budgetary framework of the Member States [8] will ensure that the objectives of the Pact are reflected in national budgetary frameworks (including accounting systems, statistics, forecasting practices, fiscal rules, budgetary procedures and fiscal relations with local or regional authorities). While taking account of Member States' specific needs and preferences, the directive sets out requirements that national budgetary frameworks should respect so as to ensure minimum quality and consistency with the EU rules.

- A regulation on the prevention and correction of macroeconomic imbalances [9], introducing the excessive imbalance procedure as a new element of the EU's economic surveillance framework. This regular assessment of the risks of imbalances will permit the Commission to launch in-depth reviews for Member States at risk. For Member States with severe imbalances or imbalances that put at risk the functioning of EMU, the Council may adopt recommendations and open an excessive imbalance procedure. A Member State would then have to present a corrective action plan that will be vetted by the Council, which will set deadlines for corrective action. Repeated failure to take corrective action will expose a euro-area Member State to sanctions.

▸ A regulation on enforcement measures to correct excessive macroeconomic imbalances in the euro area [10], under which a euro-area Member State repeatedly failing to act on Council recommendations to address excessive imbalances will have to pay a yearly fine equal to 0.1 % of its GDP. The fine can be prevented only by a qualified majority vote ('reverse voting', see above), with only euro-area Member States voting.

How the European semester will operate

In the new peer review of draft national budgets, Member States and the Commission will look at macro-financial performance as well as where the EU stands in relation to the five targets set in the Europe 2020 strategy: increasing employment; increasing research; cutting greenhouse gas emissions; improving education levels; and promoting social inclusion.

The first European semester will start in January 2011. It brings together the fiscal discipline of the Stability and Growth Pact, the structural reforms of the Europe 2020 strategy, and a new mechanism to prevent macro-imbalances. The semester aims at prior policy guidance and preventive budgetary surveillance, at a time when these matter most: budgetary policy will be discussed at EU level before budgets are agreed at national level.

The cycle will start in January with an 'annual growth survey' prepared by the Commission, reviewing economic challenges. This report will be discussed by the European Council in early spring, which will identify the main economic challenges facing the EU and give strategic advice on policies for the EU and the euro area. Taking this guidance into account, the Member States will present their medium-term budgetary strategies in their national stability and convergence programmes. At the same time, they will draw up national reform programmes setting out the action to be undertaken to strengthen their policies in areas such as employment and social inclusion. All these programmes will be issued simultaneously in April.

The Commission will then evaluate the policies set out by Member States in their programmes, and — should these not be sufficient — recommend the Council to issue country-specific policy guidance. Each July, the European Council and the Council will provide policy advice before Member States finalise their budgets for the following year. An essential aspect of the semester is that governments look at their own national reforms in related policy fields. In backing the semester, Member States have indicated that they are prepared to take ownership of this indispensable ingredient for success.

'The work on the Stability Pact is not simply about being punitive to Member States or about rectifying past mistakes ... We must not lose sight of the wider challenge of improving Europe's structural and sustainable growth rate and its general economic performance. This was the focus of the Europe 2020 strategy ... The answer to those who fear that fiscal retrenchment will cut economic growth rates is to focus better on the underlying structural factors that hinder our economic performance and to remedy them.' Herman Van Rompuy, speaking in the European Parliament, 24 November

Meanwhile, making use of the existing rules, the Commission maintained its routine surveillance of Member States' finances. During 2010, the excessive deficit procedure was initiated in 24 countries in breach of the rules, requiring them to correct their excessive deficit situation.

Budgetary expansion played a crucial role in maintaining an acceptable level of economic activity and growth. However, in order to make full use of Europe's competitive advantage, it is crucial that Member States now implement structural reforms to support private demand and innovative growth.

How EU emergency measures averted collapse

In 2009 the EU-27 countries put 9.3 % of their gross domestic product on the line to save the banking system from failure during the financial crisis.

Throughout the year, the Commission continued to authorise national state aids to banks, wherever it judged that the measure was an appropriate remedy to a serious disturbance in the national economy. This temporary support to banks allows them to ensure adequate levels of lending to companies in the real economy and helps stabilise financial markets by restoring confidence. The conditions attached ensure, at the same time, that competition is not distorted.

Altogether, between October 2008 and July 2010 the Commission approved Member State crisis measures for the banking sector with an overall maximum volume of €4 589 billion. Guarantee schemes and ad hoc interventions account for over three quarters of this volume, amounting to €3 485 billion. Between August 2008 and July 2010 the Commission approved recapitalisation measures for a volume of €546 billion. For the same period the Commission approved impaired assets interventions and liquidity measures amounting to €558 billion.

The exceptional state aid framework adopted at the beginning of the crisis, to ease some of the strains on the real economy, was extended for another year by a Commission decision in December, with new conditions attached. Once growth takes hold, exit strategies are to be put in place so that all Member States reduce support — although in a differentiated manner that reflects their varying economic and fiscal circumstances. It was recognised that Member State economies are not going to recover their dynamism or competitive edge if they rely excessively on backing from their governments. The agreement is that as from 2011, when the economic recovery is expected to have gained momentum, fiscal stance across all Member States will become more restrictive, so as to promote sustainable growth.

For the financial sector, the gradual disengagement from state support has already started. The process will occur through the tightening of conditions for new government guarantees from July 2010 through a fee increase, and through a closer scrutiny of the viability of heavy guarantee users. As of 1 January 2011, every bank in the EU having recourse to state support in the form of capital or impaired asset measures will have to submit a restructuring plan.

FINANCE AND COMPETITION AT THE SERVICE OF CITIZENS

The economic crisis revealed significant gaps in the regulatory and supervisory framework of the financial sector. Profound and comprehensive reforms have been put in place, to ensure that the financial sector is a reliable partner in the future growth of EU prosperity — and to protect the citizens and businesses that have put their trust in banks.

If the EU is to remain competitive it must champion a strong financial sector, a sector in which banks, not taxpayers, pay up front to cover the costs of their own risks of failure. Sound government finances and responsible financial markets give the confidence and economic strength for sustainable growth.

The most fundamental change is the creation of a new supervisory structure, comprising three EU authorities with binding powers over the EU's financial sector, and the creation of a European Systemic Risk Board [11]. In restoring troubled banks to health, the EU has conducted tests on their ability to withstand future shocks. And in its competition policy the EU has struck a careful balance in permitting state aid, under tight conditions, to support recovery while ensuring that the market is not distorted.

THE NEW FINANCIAL SUPERVISION ARCHITECTURE

Financial supervision took on a genuinely European dimension during the year, to match the reality that financial companies and markets operate mostly at a European level. The reform of financial supervision is unique to Europe — nowhere else in the world has such a supervisory framework been created. The new framework, adopted in November, strengthens financial sector supervision and reduces risks, making Europe a safer place economically and more attractive to investors.

For financial markets to have the confidence and trust of the public and investors, supervisory authorities need sufficient information and the power to act early when a problem arises. So the EU designed and agreed on a common approach that provides joined-up and consistent oversight of financial companies across borders.

Tough new powers have been vested in new EU-level authorities. A consensus was reached on a European supervisory structure that responds to the interests of Member States and the European Union — and above all to the needs of European citizens, consumers and investors. The new authorities can settle disputes among national financial supervisors and ban over-risky financial products and activities. And if national supervisors fail to act, then the new authorities may also impose decisions directly on financial institutions so as to remedy breaches of EU law. Attention will be focused on weak spots in financial markets, and country-by-country reporting will be introduced.

Within the new structure:

▸ Three European supervisors have been set up for the banking sector, the insurance sector, and securities trading, respectively. These micro-economic surveillance bodies replace the EU's current system of consultative committees and will have the powers necessary to ensure sound oversight across Europe, including of large, cross-border banking groups. They will adhere to a single rulebook, solving disagreements between national supervisors, monitoring the correct application of EU law and intervening in emergency situations.

▸ A completely new macro-financial surveillance body was established to monitor threats to financial stability. This so-called European Systemic Risk Board is to be chaired by the President of the ECB. It will continuously monitor threats to the EU economy and offer macro-prudential oversight of the financial system, something that had been lacking under the old system.

REFORMS TO FINANCIAL REGULATION

Reform of the financial sector was required to ensure institutions are not only well supervised but also thoroughly regulated. The financial crisis demonstrated how a lack of effective regulation created incentives for financial institutions to pursue excessive risk-taking in order to achieve short-term gains. The interconnection among financial institutions led to systemic effects with serious consequences for the entire sector. The situation was aggravated by the absence of regulation which would make possible the orderly winding up of banks without endangering financial stability.

Measures adopted to boost regulation and responsibility within the financial services sector included:

▸ a directive to regulate the activities of alternative investment fund managers [12]: hedge funds and private equity will no longer operate in a regulatory void outside the scope of supervisors. The new rules allow the marketing of funds, but subject to strict requirements, with close monitoring and supervising of risk.

▸ new requirements for the over-the-counter derivatives market [13] to avoid damaging speculation — requiring use of central clearing, logging of trades, and controls on short-selling. A taskforce is looking at the effects of naked credit default swaps on sovereign debt.

EUROPEANS CONTINUE TO OFFER THEIR SUPPORT

Europeans continue to support economic coordination between Member States, and 7 of every 10 respondents see stricter policing of the financial industry as the best way of avoiding a further crisis. These were two of the findings of a second European Parliament survey on the economic crisis, carried out by TNS Sofres between August and September 2010.

The Commission also initiated a wide range of actions to keep up the momentum of financial sector reform and to widen its scope. These proposals and consultations include:

▸ a Commission action plan ([14]) so that banks in difficulty can either be returned to health without state support, or allowed to fail without damaging the banking system as a whole. The mechanisms will be funded through levies or taxes on financial institutions. During the financial crisis, governments in the EU provided public support to financial institutions amounting to 16.5 % of EU GDP. The support was necessary to ensure the stability of the financial system, but it imposed a heavy burden on public budgets.

▸ a consultation on credit rating agencies, to re-examine the regulatory framework in the light of concerns that financial institutions and institutional investors may be relying too heavily on external ratings and do not carry out sufficient internal credit risk assessments, which may lead to volatile markets and instability of the financial system.

▸ a consultation on packaged retail investment products, aimed at raising standards of protection for customers and outlining possible measures for improving the transparency and comparability of investment products and ensuring that effective rules always govern sales.

▸ a consultation ([15]) on countercyclical capital buffers for banks, to ease fluctuations in the financial system, by ensuring that banks could draw on reserves accumulated in economically good times so as to continue lending when economic conditions worsen.

▸ a proposal for a thorough revision of the deposit guarantee schemes and investors' compensation, as well as a reorientation of insurance guarantee schemes in order to increase protection of investors and savers.

LIMITING BANKERS' BONUSES

Under new rules agreed in December ([17]), bankers will receive a maximum of a quarter of their bonuses in immediate cash payouts, with the remainder deferred or held in shares for a minimum of three years. The rules also provide for national regulators to rescind bonuses paid to senior managers whose risks were discovered to have produced losses at financial companies. The rules also seek a direct link between fixed salary and pay.

A central principle of the EU's reform of the financial system was to get more capital and capital of better quality into the system. Strengthening capital requirements should ensure that a firm has adequately addressed the risks associated with its trading book so that it reflects potential losses. The reform also seeks to ensure minimum liquidity standards, effective leverage ratios, capital sanctions for banks with irresponsible remuneration policies, and proper capital requirements for the complex financial instruments that contributed to the financial crisis. Reforms to capital requirements are not limited to Europe. Within the Basel Committee on Banking Supervision, the European Union is negotiating with international partners. These reforms are being implemented in the EU through amendments ([16]) to the capital requirements directive.

Overall, these measures help to keep EU markets attractive, and to ensure that the European economy has the means to promote growth. But financial regulation is also about improving the daily life of European citizens, simplifying their everyday lives and bringing them the transparency and security that they should expect from Europe.

COMPETITION POLICY SHAPING RESPONSES

Competition policy, and in particular the coherent and predictable enforcement of state aid rules, played an important role in the response to the crisis. Extraordinary rescue measures adopted at the beginning of the crisis proved successful as they were capable of restoring financial stability and of supporting economic recovery. State aid policy has helped shape governments' responses to the crisis and also prevented a meltdown of the financial system. This avoided subsidy races between Member States, reduced distortions of competition and limited the incentives for excessive risk-taking. The Commission decisions facilitated access to credit and provided a mechanism for the coordination of Member States' bailouts of financial institutions.

The Commission has also explicitly tackled moral hazard. This arises when a company believes it can behave irresponsibly with impunity, convinced that it will be protected from failure because its collapse would provoke unacceptably wide repercussions for society. It is for this reason that the Commission ensured that aid was not granted as a mere gift to failing businesses, but that all bailouts come with conditions — a prerequisite for a return to normal functioning of the market. Following the initial rescue stage, aid notified to the Commission was cleared on the express condition that the restructuring plans or viability reviews of banks receiving aid were to be approved by the Commission. There were often requirements attached to these restructuring plans, for example regarding divestitures or behaviour on the market post-restructuring. Loans and guarantees were granted on the same terms and on the basis of the same European-wide rules. The EU economy and EU taxpayers are better off as a result. The measures helped financial institutions regain viability. The Commission also adjusted its rules on state guarantees to the banking sector so as to signal to banks that they have to get ready for a disengagement from exceptional crisis-related state support.

As from the start of 2011, new measures extend the requirement for restructuring plans to every bank in the EU having recourse to state support in the form of capital or impaired asset measures, and a new state aid framework for rescue and restructuring of banks is under development, to be followed by a review of the general rescue and restructuring guidelines for firms in difficulty.

Tangible competition measures for recovery

▶ Maintaining a level-playing field across Europe — such as ensuring that aid to the automotive sector does not impose any conditions on location

▶ Preventing bankruptcies through the temporary framework allowing Member States to provide access to finance to viable firms, prolonged for 2011 with limited scope, stricter conditions and a focus on small and medium-sized enterprises (SMEs)

▶ Support for 'smart investments' — such as through the 'State aid broadband guidelines' — to help economic recovery in the short run and bring long-term benefits for European competitiveness.

Competition encourages companies to adapt their business strategies, to innovate and to create better products and services. In turn, this leads to providing consumers with more choice, better quality and lower prices. The application of an EU-wide competition policy ensures that no matter where businesses are located, they have access to the same opportunities across Europe. Competition policy drives innovation and growth by keeping markets open and competitive, so that businesses have the opportunity to prosper and consumers can reap the benefits.

To ensure that consumers have more choice and can benefit from more advantageous prices, the Commission adopted a regulation that exempts a wide range of agreements between manufacturers and distributors for the sale of products and services [18]. Companies with a modest presence on the market remain free to decide how their products are distributed as long as they avoid behaviour obviously harmful for consumers and competition, such as price fixing. Together with the accompanying guidelines [19], the regulation aims at promoting Internet distribution, entitling approved distributors to sell on the Internet without limitation on quantities, customers' location or prices.

In the energy sector, modification of the environmental guidelines on state aid is intended to help the emissions trading system become a tool for low-cost compliance and an incentive for investments in low-carbon technologies. The regulation on state aid in the coal sector [20] — where Member States need to be able to continue support to the industry as long as coal maintains its major role in energy production in Europe — aims to assure fair competition by authorising aid for closure and for inherited costs.

The Commission intervened to ensure that planned national aids to the automotive sector respected state aid and single market rules. And it decided to end certain special provisions introduced during the crisis to allow Member States to provide emergency access to finance to prevent businesses from going bankrupt.

© European Union

The car industry remains an important sector in the EU economy.

GLOBAL RECOVERY AND INTERNATIONAL COOPERATION

The EU operates in a globalised world. One of the EU's main functions in this wider context is to shape global responses in the interest of its Member States and citizens. Economic downturns in the past have led to vicious circles of protectionism, subsidy races and worse. Getting the world economy back on track towards growth and prosperity requires global leadership and multilateral action. In this, the EU cannot act alone, and cannot build a regulatory reform agenda in isolation.

The EU took a leading role in promoting international responses to the crisis. It was prominent in discussions within the G20, the premier forum for international economic cooperation, where the EU is represented by Commission President José Manuel Barroso and European Council President Herman Van Rompuy. At successive meetings the EU argued for global efforts to fill in the gaps in financial regulation and supervision at international level. It took a leading role in promoting new rules on bank capital. It kept up pressure for effective action to plug deficits and reduce debt while stimulating growth prospects. And it pushed strongly for a global agreement on bank levies and taxes. Moreover, in order to ensure that trade could continue to play its role in economic recovery, the European Union played a pivotal role in monitoring major economies' compliance with their commitment, made at the G20, not to introduce new barriers to free trade.

The most important event of 2010 in this respect was the G20 summit in Seoul in November, where the EU made progress in promoting joint action to boost global growth and jobs. A 'Seoul action plan' (^{21}) commits the G20 further to global action for balanced growth, and is a clear recognition of joint responsibility under which all major economies have agreed to do their part to achieve rebalancing to tackle imbalances. The EU method of using indicators to trigger an assessment of macroeconomic imbalances and their root causes was backed by the G20 leaders. The EU also helped to build a consensus on cooperative solutions to tensions on currency issues and trade. Leaders agreed to move to more market-based exchange rates and enhance exchange rate flexibility to reflect underlying economic fundamentals and refrain from competitive devaluations — as EU leaders had called for in advance of the summit. By endorsing the Basel III reform, the G20 also kept up the momentum for global financial regulatory reform, a key priority for the EU.

The leaders of Germany, France, Italy, and the United Kingdom, together with European Council President Herman Van Rompuy and European Commission President José Manuel Barroso, take part in the G8 summit in Canada in June, along with the leaders of the United States, Canada, Japan and Russia.

© Peer Grimm / DPA / Reporters

BASEL III

Basel III is a comprehensive set of reform measures developed by the Basel Committee on Banking Supervision to strengthen the regulation, supervision and risk management of the banking sector. It aims to improve the banking sector's ability to absorb shocks, refine risk management and governance, and strengthen banks' transparency. It targets regulation both at the level of individual banks and system-wide across the sector. The Basel III reforms are part of the global initiatives to strengthen the financial regulatory system that have been endorsed by G20 leaders, and implementation is envisaged in 2012.

The EU secured a valuable commitment at the G20 summit in Seoul to fight protectionism in all its forms. The Commission also produced a series of protectionist reports naming and shaming offenders, as part of a concerted effort to keep economies open and prevent intensification of the effects of the crisis. The 'Trade, growth and world affairs' communication ([22]) in November set out an assertive trade policy agenda for the next five years, as the external plank of the EU's bid to revitalise Europe's economy, complementing major initiatives during the year on the internal market and on industry and innovation. It proposes a strategy to reduce trade barriers, to open global markets and to get a fair deal for European businesses. The overall aim is to ensure the benefits of trade reach European citizens — in the form of stronger economic growth, more jobs and increased consumer choice at lower prices.

THE EUROPE 2020 STRATEGY — SMART, SUSTAINABLE AND INCLUSIVE GROWTH

Sound public finances, tighter financial supervision and open world markets are means to an end: growth for jobs in the EU. The structural measures under the Europe 2020 strategy tackle the underlying causes of the crisis. They are part of the EU's comprehensive strategy to create a more sustainable and dynamic growth path delivering high levels of employment, productivity and social cohesion. The goal is smart growth, sustainable growth, inclusive growth.

To counter the risks from strained public finances, dented business confidence and the threat of unemployment, the EU proposed a series of actions over the course of 2010 to invigorate the economy, to unlock the EU's growth potential, stimulate investment and upgrade skills. The EU put emphasis on low energy use, low carbon emissions, up-skilling its population, seizing the potential of a digital single market, research and development and advanced technology. This is the way Europe will boost its competitiveness and productivity, and promote social cohesion and economic convergence.

Smart, sustainable and inclusive growth is the aim of the Europe 2020 strategy. Smart growth refers to fostering knowledge, innovation, education and the digital society. Sustainable growth means making production more resource efficient while boosting competitiveness. And inclusive growth targets raising participation in the labour market, increasing the acquisition of skills and tackling poverty.

European Commission President José Manuel Barroso launched the Europe 2020 strategy for smart, sustainable and inclusive growth, in March.

The Europe 2020 strategy provides a coherent framework for the Union to mobilise all its instruments and policies to secure the structural reforms that Europe needs. It sets five specific targets to be achieved by 2020. It encourages closer engagement of Member States in delivering, since ownership is crucial to the success of the strategy. The specific targets are amplified by a series of flagship initiatives, and by integrated guidelines for economic and employment policies [23]. The strategy is complemented by the EU's continued development of the single market and the pursuit of smarter regulation and a stimulating environment for competition. But equally important is the goal of creating an ever-more inclusive society, which is why social cohesion and social inclusion are at the heart of the Europe 2020 strategy.

STABILISING UNEMPLOYMENT LEVELS ACROSS THE EU

Unemployment (%) in the 27 EU countries 2010–12 are forecasts

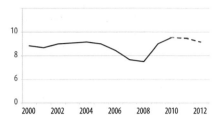

Source: European Commission.

The five specific targets of the Europe 2020 strategy: concrete objectives

▸ Raising the employment rate for women and men aged 20–64 to 75 %, with more young, older and low-skilled workers in jobs, and better integration of legal migrants.

▸ Improving the conditions for research and development so as to raise investment levels to 3 % of GDP, and stimulating R & D and innovation with new indicators.

▸ Cutting greenhouse gas emissions by 20 % compared with 1990 levels — at the same time maintaining the EU's conditional commitment to a 30 % emissions reduction by 2020; raising the share of renewables in final energy consumption to 20 %; and moving towards a 20 % increase in energy efficiency.

▸ Improving education levels, by reducing school dropout rates below 10 % and increasing to 40 % the proportion of 30- to 34-year-olds with tertiary or equivalent qualifications.

▸ Promoting social inclusion, through reducing poverty, and lifting at least 20 million people out of the risk of poverty and exclusion.

UNLEASHING EUROPE'S POTENTIAL — THE SEVEN FLAGSHIPS

The first flagship to be unveiled, in May, was the **digital agenda for Europe** [24] — Europe's strategy for a flourishing digital economy by 2020. This is a sector that can deliver smart growth. Half of European productivity growth over the last 15 years was driven by information and communication technologies. This trend is set to intensify. The digital agenda will deliver a single digital market worth 4 % of EU GDP by 2020.

The 100 actions of the digital agenda aim to spread the benefits of the digital revolution. It will promote a digital single market, extend Internet access, help make devices and applications more interoperable, boost trust in the Internet by enhancing security and protecting privacy for citizens and businesses and leveraging investment in ICT research and innovation.

THE SEVEN FLAGSHIPS OF THE EUROPE 2020 STRATEGY

▸ The digital agenda for Europe

▸ The innovation union

▸ Youth on the move

▸ Resource efficiency

▸ An industrial policy for the globalisation era

▸ An agenda for new skills and jobs

▸ The European Platform against Poverty and Social Exclusion

Training in digital literacy skills is central to the Europe 2020 strategy.

The Commission has launched a public consultation on how best to unlock the full potential of Europe's cultural and creative industries. It is already focusing on improving access to finance, especially for small businesses, to enable the sector to flourish and to contribute to sustainable and inclusive growth. Improvements in mutual recognition of how to deal with material whose potential right-holders are unknown — orphan works — will ease cross-border online accessibility and make Europe's cultural and intellectual heritage more widely available. Clearer rules on collective rights management will provide a stable framework to increase cross-border services and encourage offers for an online audiovisual market. Online distribution of audiovisual works and other creative content is to be stimulated.

Investment in next-generation fibre broadband network is being promoted, particularly through bringing new clarity to the industry on competition rules. Complementary measures ([25]) reflect the commitments in the digital agenda to provide every European with access to basic broadband by 2013 and fast and ultra-fast broadband by 2020. Other components of the digital agenda include enhancing digital literacy skills and promoting broader inclusion — overcoming the 'digital divide' so that background or lack of skills do not limit participation. In December the Commission launched its eGovernment action plan for better online services to citizens and businesses. It will help the EU achieve the commitment in the digital agenda to deliver innovative online public services and increase the take-up of these services.

Other flagship initiatives emerged later in the year, all linked to the idea of boosting wealth and jobs while protecting the environment and making the EU more inclusive.

Europe's innovation performance needs to be improved along the whole supply chain, from research to retail, notably through innovation partnerships. This is why the Commission proposed — and the European Council endorsed — an **innovation union** [26]. This is the first comprehensive strategy for innovation. It aims to improve conditions and access to funding for research and innovation in Europe, to ensure that innovative ideas can be turned into products and services that create growth and jobs. It focuses on areas of major concern for citizens, such as climate change, energy efficiency and healthy living. It looks at innovation not only in terms of technology, but also in relation to the business models, design, branding and services that add value for users. Furthermore, the flagship includes public sector and social innovation as well as commercial innovation, aiming to involve all actors and all regions in the innovation cycle. The objective is that Europe should be a world-class science performer, with close public and private sector cooperation. Attention is also focused on helping ideas to get quickly to market, by removing bottlenecks like expensive patenting, market fragmentation, slow standard-setting and skill shortages. Achieving the target of investing 3 % of EU GDP in R & D by 2020 could create 3.7 million jobs and increase annual GDP by €795 billion by 2025. This would mean Europe would require at least 1 million more researchers in the next decade.

Within the innovation strategy, European innovation partnerships will bring together European, national and regional, public and private actors behind well-defined goals in areas which combine tackling societal challenges with potential for Europe to become a world leader. The Commission will provide seed funding to attract further finance. Further down the line, as from 2011, pilot partnerships will be launched on active and healthy ageing, energy, 'smart' cities and mobility, water efficiency, non-energy raw materials and sustainable and productive agriculture.

The strategy is flanked and reinforced by input from other EU policies. Competition policy will support initiatives that drive innovation and growth by ensuring a level playing field exists between companies and allowing them to compete based on their merits. Under its research programmes, the Commission will invest some €500 million in exploratory research in future and emerging technologies, and will urge Member States to do the same. The European Institute for Innovation and Technology launched its first three knowledge and innovation communities in June. These stimulate innovation and entrepreneurship in climate change mitigation and adaptation, sustainable energy, and the future information and communication society. The seventh framework programme for research and technological development will play its part: the indicative budget for 2010 is over €6 billion, which will fund thousands of projects and create more than 165 000 jobs. The Commission also developed new joint research programming initiatives in agriculture, food security and climate change; cultural heritage and global change; and a healthy diet for a healthy life.

SUCCESSES IN EUROPEAN RESEARCH SUPPORT

In December the Marie Curie Actions programme funded its 50 000th researcher since its 1996 launch. To achieve an innovative union, Europe needs world-class researchers who are able to tackle both current and future challenges, and the EU is committed to inspiring, motivating, training and retaining them. By supporting the mobility of researchers across a wide range of disciplines, both in industry and academia, the Marie Curie Actions contribute to the European Union's objective of creating a strong labour market for highly skilled, creative and entrepreneurial researchers.

RESEARCH FUNDING

In 2010, the EU launched the first joint programming initiative, on neurodegenerative diseases — such as Alzheimer's disease. European countries choosing to participate in a joint programming initiative pool their resources and coordinate their efforts to increase the efficiency of public research funding and avoid duplication of efforts. They draft a strategic research agenda and an implementation plan to give a joint response to a shared challenge.

Youth on the move [27], launched in September, brings together EU and national measures to improve employment prospects for young people, students and trainees. It aims at raising the quality of all levels of education and training, and offering more opportunities to young people to study and train abroad. It will provide greater mobility for participants in university and research programmes, promote entrepreneurship among young professionals, and boost recognition of informal learning. Actions include an improved European job portal, more help for public employment services to support young people, and a pilot project that allows young entrepreneurs to spend up to six months with an experienced entrepreneur in a smaller firm in another EU Member State.

The European Union has already agreed extra budget provision from 2011 for a pilot scheme to help young people seize the opportunities in the wider EU labour market, and to help companies find qualified workers. And the new European Progress Microfinance Facility will make it easier for young entrepreneurs to access credit. The Commission has called on Member States to strongly resist cuts to education budgets as part of austerity measures in response to the crisis.

In June, the Commission proposed a 10-year vision for improving vocational education and training, and new education targets were endorsed by the European Council. The European higher education area was launched in March, which aims to make European higher education more compatible, comparable, competitive and attractive.

The 'Youth on the move' initiative also looks at policies which could cushion the impact of the crisis on young people. These include making easier transitions from education and training to work, and better links between policy priorities and EU funds, especially the European Social Fund. It also envisaged increased direct support to innovative projects through Progress, the lifelong learning and 'Youth in action' programmes.

In October the Commission insisted, in its communication 'An integrated **industrial policy for the globalisation era**' [28], that industry must be placed centre stage if Europe is to remain a global economic leader. This flagship initiative sets out a strategy that aims to boost growth and jobs by maintaining and supporting a strong, diversified and competitive industrial base in Europe offering well-paid jobs while becoming less carbon intensive.

Against the background of intensifying globalisation, this new approach discards the obsolete concept of national sectors and industries in favour of a coordinated European policy response. This requires a vision of the whole value chain, from infrastructure and raw materials to after-sales service. It places the creation and growth of small and medium-sized enterprises at the core of industrial policy, and seizes the transition to a sustainable economy as an opportunity to strengthen competitiveness.

Altogether the EU set aside more than €1.1 billion to ease access to loans and equity finance for smaller firms, especially new and young firms and people wanting to start their own business. The European Investment Bank also provided special assistance to smaller firms, with accelerated delivery of loans to them resulting in almost full utilisation of the €30 billion allocation for 2008–11. The focus is on clean transport, renewable energy and related research.

Small and medium-sized enterprises are at the heart of the EU's recovery. Here apprentices learn new skills at a college in the United Kingdom.

There were striking developments in numerous industrial sectors in the EU in 2010. The Commission proposed ([29]) initiatives to promote the competitiveness of tourism, and its development and international visibility. The Commission proposed in April 2010 a shift in policy on vehicle manufacturing, to encourage the development and eventual widespread use of clean and energy efficient vehicles. The chemical industry moved towards further competitiveness, with the submission to the European Chemicals Agency of 24 675 registrations of the most widely used or most dangerous chemicals by the deadline of 30 November.

UNEMPLOYED IN THE EU COUNTRIES

Unemployment rate (%)

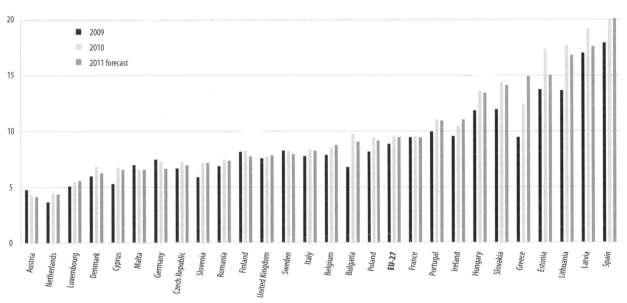

- 2009
- 2010
- 2011 forecast

Austria, Netherlands, Luxembourg, Denmark, Cyprus, Malta, Germany, Czech Republic, Slovenia, Romania, Finland, United Kingdom, Sweden, Italy, Belgium, Bulgaria, Poland, EU-27, France, Portugal, Ireland, Hungary, Slovakia, Greece, Estonia, Lithuania, Latvia, Spain

Source: European Commission.

The 'Enterprise Europe' network gives Europe's smaller firms easier access to export markets. With 589 partner organisations covering 47 countries, it is extending its reach, particularly into Asia: it now has 15 contact points in China and South Korea, with additional contact points planned in China and Japan.

An agenda for new skills and jobs will boost inclusive growth by raising the employment rate with more and better jobs. It aims to help people of all ages anticipate and manage change through equipping them with the right skills and competences. Its scope also includes modernisation of labour markets and welfare systems and aims to ensure that the benefits of growth reach all parts of the EU. Among the specific mechanisms envisaged are labour market reforms to improve flexicurity, a single contract instead of different models of temporary and permanent contracts, new impetus to lifelong learning, additional incentives for firms to invest in training, and better foresight on future skills needs. It proposes a shared interface — European skills, competences and occupations classification — to bring more closely together the worlds of employment, education and training.

The European Platform against Poverty and Social Exclusion was launched in December. It will promote innovation in social policy to find smart solutions in post-crisis Europe, especially in terms of more effective and efficient social support. It urges making the best use of all EU funds, in particular the European Social Fund, to support social inclusion objectives, and it proposes social policy as a priority for future EU funding. It aims to make social protection and services more effective and responsive to new social needs. And it will bring on board a wider range of partners to fight exclusion.

The 2010 European Year for Combating Poverty and Social Exclusion

With a total budget of €17 million (complemented by at least €9 million of national co-financing), the European Year for Combating Poverty and Social Exclusion supported more than 700 projects across 29 countries. The political momentum generated paved the way for the agreement by EU leaders on the first-ever poverty reduction target within the Europe 2020 strategy. The events included a Europe-wide competition for journalists reporting on issues linked to the year's themes, and national initiatives ranging from broadcasts, on Ireland's biggest radio station, of stories of people living in poverty, to helping 60 communities in the Netherlands to develop integrated strategies for tackling social exclusion, and from German help for disadvantaged people with a migrant background to integrate in society through local volunteering, to training job centre staff in Denmark so they can deal better with the specific needs of people with mental disabilities seeking work.

Regional policy

Under cohesion policy, €93 billion (27 % of EU funding earmarked for 2007–13) has already been allocated to projects for investment in jobs and growth in Europe, with progress in key sectors such as R & D and innovation particularly advanced, and positive results from the training and up-skilling offered by the European Social Fund to job-seekers. Through the European Regional Development Fund, the European Social Fund and the Cohesion Fund, the EU will invest €347 billion in 2007–13 in the 27 Member States.

EU cohesion policy contributed to growth and prosperity and to promoting balanced development across the Union, both through direct investments and indirect trade benefits. It also helped to cushion the impact of the crisis on workers and small businesses. The Commission urged [30] aligning it still more closely to the Europe 2020 strategy, to help address new challenges arising from the substantial economic and social developments over recent years. The recommendations covered stricter conditions, greater incentives and increased focus on results.

At a regional level, citizens benefited from action such as the development of the EU strategy for the Danube region, presented in December, which seeks to improve environmental conditions and develop the huge economic potential of the region and to overcome the social and infrastructure disparities that still persist from the region's divided past. The strategy will help eradicate this unequal legacy, boosting opportunities for its citizens through enhanced trade, transport and energy networks, promoting innovation in smaller firms, and through cultural and educational activities.

The **resource efficiency flagship** will not be launched until early in 2011, but related actions are already under way. For example, sustainable transport is being pursued through: earlier funding of the trans-European transport network; faster reform of the single European sky; implementation of the European maritime transport space without barriers, to promote transport by sea; improved global competitiveness through higher productivity; and simplified access to structural funding. A number of these issues will be dealt with in more detail in Chapter 2. The Council welcomed the resource efficiency flagship initiative in December [31] and, in particular, progress towards a sustainable life-cycle approach, the blend of measures that will be needed to make European material use more sustainable.

GREEN SECTOR EMPLOYMENT

Green industries already directly employ around 3.4 million people and account for around 2.2 % of Europe's GDP. Each direct job in Europe's eco-industries creates between 1.3 and 1.9 indirect jobs. The global market for environmental technologies is forecast to grow around 10 % annually in future. Some 3 million more green EU jobs could be created.

Maintenance of photovoltaic cells at the world's largest roof solar power station, in Germany.

© Nestor Bachmann / DPA / Reporters

RELAUNCHING THE SINGLE MARKET

Improving the single market is a pillar of the Europe 2020 strategy and a prerequisite for its success. In October the Commission set out its plans ([32]) to strengthen the single market with measures to boost growth and enhance citizens' rights. To boost growth, competitiveness and social progress, it made proposals to make the single market work better, and make life easier for companies, consumers and workers. The Single Market Act is a comprehensive two-year plan for 2011–12 designed to relaunch growth and create jobs in the EU. It contains 50 initiatives relating to economics, governance and the general public. Key priorities include:

▶ For businesses: Gaining access to finance can be difficult for SMEs. The Commission plans to make proposals increasing the visibility of Europe's smallest businesses and easing their access to lists for capital markets. These proposals will also reduce costs for SMEs by simplifying accounting rules and improving their access to public procurement contracts. The Commission will look at introducing a common tax base for businesses operating cross-border, leading to further cost savings.

▶ For businesses: Europe has enormous potential for developing social entrepreneurship. In recent years, many initiatives have been taken by individuals, foundations and companies to improve access to food, housing, healthcare, jobs and banking services for those in need. To foster more cross-border action, the Commission will propose European statutes for such organisations to serve and promote the social economy. The Commission will also encourage longer term investments, including ethical investments, exploring options for a specific labelling regime.

▶ For consumers: Today, the online market is seriously underperforming. That is why the Commission will propose rules in 2011 aimed at ensuring that creators and artists can sell their work throughout Europe with a one-stop shop for authorisation allowing them to reap the rewards of their work. Full implementation of the services directive and updated rules for e-commerce will also make a difference.

▶ For employees: 4 600 professions are regulated differently in Member States. A thorough revision of the professional qualifications directive is therefore overdue. The Commission believes introduction of professional ID cards or *cartes professionnelles* would reduce remaining red tape.

The Commission's initiative for a Single Market Act follows the delivery in May, by former Internal Market and Competition Commissioner Mario Monti, of a report on how the EU should relaunch and complete the single market, which had been requested in October 2009 by Commission President Barroso. The June European Council welcomed the report. A European Parliament report on delivering a single market to consumers and citizens was adopted at the May plenary ([33]).

THE SINGLE MARKET AWARD

In December the 2010 Single Market Award went to the Austrian NGO 'Grenzoffensive'. This prize highlights the importance of free movement principles underpinning the EU single market. Grenzoffensive won for its work in minimising administrative obstacles for workers and small and medium-sized enterprises working across borders in the neighbouring regions of Bavaria (Germany), Upper Austria, and Southern Bohemia (Czech Republic).

In December the Council endorsed ([34]) the approach — in particular, the focus on business and citizens' concerns that prevent them from taking full benefit of the advantages of the single market. It welcomed the Commission's communication, and underlined that the single market should focus on boosting competitiveness and smart, sustainable and inclusive growth, as well as on restoring and strengthening the confidence of citizens and consumers, by putting them at the heart of the single market, and the confidence of businesses in their access to the single market.

There is no single solution to creating an EU that is fit for success in the 21st century. Reinforcing fiscal and financial stability is vital, and so too is the vision in the Europe 2020 strategy. But success comes from mobilising all the EU's many assets and facets to build a new and sustainable form of growth. The EU deployed with renewed vigour and precision its policies on the single market, competition and cohesion. It helped Member States outside the euro area (Latvia, Hungary and Romania) with balance of payments support. And it developed and exploited new forms of cooperation among the EU institutions. The year 2010 saw the EU act with new coherence to provide a genuinely comprehensive approach.

© European Union

Mr Mario Monti, former Internal Market and Competition Commissioner.

EU instruments are already having a positive impact

The European Globalisation Adjustment Fund, which supports workers dismissed as a result of globalisation and the economic crisis, granted €52.3 million in 2009 to help some 11 000 workers in eight countries. Payments were approved to Ireland, Spain, Denmark, the Netherlands and Portugal, and access rules were eased. The fund co-finances job-search assistance, training and retraining, and support for business creation. It has a high success rate in helping find new jobs.

The European Progress Microfinance Facility[35], agreed in March, is helping people to stay in jobs or to get new ones. It provides loans to people who have lost their jobs and want to start their own small business, but who do not have conventional credit records. Its starting budget is €100 million, which could leverage more than €500 million in cooperation with international financial institutions such as the European Investment Bank.

The prospects of combating late payment in commercial transactions improved when the European Parliament voted in October in favour of a new directive that will give better protection to creditors, particularly the many small firms that depend on prompt payment to safeguard their cashflow. Public authorities will have to pay within 30 days, or else pay an interest rate of 8 % — resulting in an extra €180 billion of liquidity being available to businesses.

To ease access to finance for small businesses, the EU deployed its enterprise and innovation programme, and its SME Finance Forum brought together banks, business organisations and other interested parties to discuss how the flow of finance to businesses can be improved.

Rules governing the structural and cohesion funds were simplified in June, facilitating access to funding — particularly valuable at a time when pressure on public budgets makes it more difficult for governments and regions to provide matching funding. Speeding up project implementation on the ground by reducing red tape also helps national and regional economies to recover.

ENDNOTES

(¹) Commission communication — Europe 2020 — A strategy for smart, sustainable and inclusive growth (COM(2010) 2020).

(²) Statement of the Heads of State or Government of the euro area (PCE 86/10 of 7 May 2010) (http://www.consilium.europa.eu/uedocs/cms_data/docs/pressdata/en/ec/114296.pdf).

(³) Extraordinary Economic and Financial Affairs Council conclusions, 9/10 May 2010 (http://www.consilium.europa.eu/uedocs/cms_data/docs/pressdata/en/ecofin/114324.pdf).

(⁴) 6/7 December Eurogroup/Ecofin Council.

(⁵) Commission communication — Reinforcing economic policy coordination (COM(2010) 250).

(⁶) Proposal for a regulation on speeding up and clarifying the implementation of the excessive deficit procedure (COM(2010) 522).

(⁷) Proposal for a regulation on the effective enforcement of budgetary surveillance in the euro area (COM(2010) 524).

(⁸) Proposal for a directive on requirements for budgetary frameworks of the Member States (COM(2010) 523).

(⁹) Proposal for a regulation on prevention and correction of macroeconomic imbalances (COM(2010) 527).

(¹⁰) Proposal for a regulation on enforcement measures to correct excessive macroeconomic imbalances in the euro area (COM(2010) 525).

(¹¹) Proposal for a regulation on Community macro prudential oversight of the financial system and establishing a European Systemic Risk Board (COM(2009) 499).

(¹²) Directive on alternative investment funds managers (AIFM), voted through by the EP on 11 November, awaiting Council adoption.

(¹³) Proposal for a regulation on OTC derivatives, central counterparties and trade repositories (COM(2010) 484).

(¹⁴) Commission communication — An EU framework for crisis management in the financial sector (COM(2010) 579).

(¹⁵) http://ec.europa.eu/internal_market/bank/regcapital/index_en.htm

(¹⁶) http://europa.eu/rapid/pressReleasesAction.do?reference=MEMO/10/304&format=HTML&aged=0&language=EN&guiLanguage=en

(¹⁷) Committee of European Banking Supervisors, 10 December.

(¹⁸) Commission Regulation (EU) No 330/2010 on the application of Article 101(3) of the Treaty on the Functioning of the European Union to categories of vertical agreements and concerted practices (OJ L 102, 23.4.2010).

(¹⁹) Guidelines on vertical restraints (OJ C 130, 19.5.2010).

(²⁰) Proposal for a regulation on state aid to facilitate the closure of uncompetitive coal mines (COM(2010) 372).

(²¹) Multi-year action plan on development (http://www.g20.utoronto.ca/2010/g20seoul-development.pdf).

(²²) Commission communication — Trade, growth and world affairs — Trade policy as a core component of the EU's 2020 strategy (COM(2010) 612).

(²³) Council Decision 2010/707/EU on guidelines for the employment policies of the Member States (OJ L 308, 24.11.2010).

(²⁴) Commission communication — A digital agenda for Europe (COM(2010) 245).

(²⁵) Commission Recommendation 2010/572/EU on regulated access to Next Generation Access Networks (NGA) (OJ L 251, 25.9.2010).
Proposal for a decision establishing the first radio spectrum policy programme (COM(2010) 471).
Commission communication — European broadband: Investing in digitally driven growth (COM(2010) 472).

(²⁶) Commission communication — Europe 2020 flagship initiative — Innovation union (COM(2010) 546).

(²⁷) Commission communication — Youth on the move — An initiative to unleash the potential of young people to achieve smart, sustainable and inclusive growth in the European Union (COM(2010) 477).

(²⁸) Commission communication — An integrated industrial policy for the globalisation era — Putting competitiveness and sustainability at centre stage (COM(2010) 614).

(²⁹) Commission communication — Europe, the world's No 1 tourist destination — A new political framework for tourism in Europe (COM(2010) 352).

(³⁰) Commission's fifth report on economic, social and territorial cohesion, 10 November, (http://ec.europa.eu/regional_policy/cohesion_report).

(³¹) 20 December Environment Council conclusions.

(³²) Commission communication — Towards a Single Market Act (COM(2010) 608).

(³³) European Parliament report of 3 May 2010 on delivering a single market to consumers and citizens (http://www.europarl.europa.eu/sides/getDoc.do?language=EN&reference=A7-0132/2010).

(³⁴) http://www.consilium.europa.eu/uedocs/cms_data/docs/pressdata/en/intm/118409.pdf

(³⁵) Decision 283/2010/EU establishing a European Progress Microfinance Facility for employment and social inclusion (OJ L 87, 7.4.2010).

**CHAPTER 2
A CITIZENS' AGENDA:
PUTTING PEOPLE AT THE HEART
OF EUROPEAN ACTION**

The aim of the Commission's Europe 2020 strategy for growth and jobs, adopted in March 2010, is ultimately to benefit European citizens. The Treaty of Lisbon, in force since December 2009, had already signalled this shift. The interests of the citizen and the democratic legitimacy of the Union have been enhanced through the increased role of the European Parliament as co-legislator in most areas and the greater involvement of national parliaments, making the EU more accountable for its actions. Secondly, the introduction of qualified majority voting in the Council for most policy areas will streamline decision-making. And finally, judicial review will be improved as the Court of Justice of the European Union is now assuming judicial oversight of all aspects of freedom security and justice, while the Charter of Fundamental Rights becomes legally binding on the EU.

By paving the way for making the EU more efficient, democratic and accountable, the treaty gives additional attention to the interests of the citizens of the EU, placing them more firmly than ever at the centre of the EU's activities and goals. The citizens' initiative is an obvious example of this new focus.

At the start of the Commission's mandate earlier in the year, President Barroso created two new portfolios: one explicitly dedicated to justice, fundamental rights and citizenship, which he entrusted to one of his Vice-Presidents — a clear policy signal recognising the key importance of EU action in this area. The other portfolio, home affairs, includes the important and delicate task of ensuring that all activities necessary and beneficial to the economic, cultural and social growth of the EU may develop in a lawful and secure environment. It also covers all activities related to the management of migratory flows, protection to people fleeing from persecution and the controls at the external borders.

One of the most prominent aspects of the new focus on citizens is to make benefits more tangible in the area of freedom, security and justice. Actions in this area are embodied in the Stockholm programme, which places the main focus on the interests and needs of citizens and addresses the necessity of ensuring respect for fundamental freedoms and integrity while guaranteeing security. Substantial progress was made over the course of the year in bringing the programme to fruition and to first concrete results.

The EU continues to meet people's concerns and interests through measures across a wide range of policy fields affecting their daily life, from health and education to culture and transport, and from consumer rights to civil protection.

AN AREA OF FREEDOM, SECURITY AND JUSTICE FOR CITIZENS

In December 2009, the European Council adopted the 'Stockholm programme — An open and secure Europe serving and protecting the citizens' (¹). It covers actions in the areas of fundamental rights, civil and criminal justice, consumer rights and citizenship, security, asylum, immigration and border management. It also sets the political guidelines for further developing the area of freedom, security and justice over the next five years. In April, the Commission adopted an action plan (²) to turn the concept into reality, translating the political guidance provided by the European Council and by the European Parliament (³) into concrete actions with a clear timetable and deliverables.

Under the Commission's action plan, the main thrust of the European Union's action in this field in the coming years will be to make real progress towards a Europe where people can live, work and travel in security, confident that their rights are fully respected. As regards fundamental rights and justice, the Commission's action plan includes the following proposals:

▸ improving **data protection** for citizens in all EU policies — including law enforcement and crime prevention — and in relations with international partners, notably with the USA; the 1995 EU data protection directive will be modernised to respond to new technological challenges;

▸ strengthening the **rights of suspects and accused persons in criminal proceedings** to have a fair trial with proposals on informing them about charges, providing legal advice, communicating with relatives and ensuring special safeguards for vulnerable persons;

▸ **cutting red tape for citizens and businesses** by ensuring that judicial decisions and civil documents are recognised across borders without cumbersome procedures or excessive costs;

▸ simplifying the **cross-border recovery of debt and alternative dispute resolution**; today companies only recover 37 % of cross-border debts;

▸ boosting online commerce by offering companies an **optional European contract law**: in 2008 only 7 % of transactions on the Internet in Europe were cross-border;

▸ increasing protection for citizens travelling outside their home countries in the EU when they book a **holiday package** or file a claim after a road accident. For travel outside the EU, citizens will have better **consular protection**.

To ensure European citizens' security and a better management of migration flows, the Stockholm action plan foresees the following proposals:

▸ defining a comprehensive EU internal **security strategy** targeting the most urgent security threats facing Europe;

▸ negotiating a long-term agreement with the USA on the processing and **transfer of financial messaging data** for the purpose of fighting terrorism (Terrorism Financing Tracking Programme — TFTP);

▸ looking at an EU approach for the use of **passenger name record (EU-PNR) data** for law enforcement purposes and creating a European framework for the communication of PNR data to non-EU countries;

- protecting European citizens from **cybercrime by criminalising identity theft** as well as malicious software that is used to attack information systems;

- reinforcing border security by setting up an **entry/exit system**, facilitating non-EU country nationals' travel through a **'registered traveller programme'** and looking at a European approach for a **European electronic system for travel authorisation** (EU ESTA);

- evaluating and, if necessary, amending the **data retention directive**;

- clearing the conditions of entry and residence of **non-EU nationals** for purposes of **seasonal employment** and intra-corporate transfers, introducing a **common EU asylum system** and fostering solidarity between Member States;

- protecting children from sexual exploitation and child pornography, in particular in view of the development of the Internet and the facilitation of international travel;

- fighting modern slavery more effectively by enhancing the criminalisation of traffickers and strengthening the protection for victims of trafficking in human beings;

- ensuring that crime does not pay and depriving criminals of the assets they have acquired through more effective asset confiscation.

The citizens' initiative: under the provisions in the Treaty of Lisbon, citizens have gained new rights to seek a voice in EU policies.

A greater say for Europe's citizens: the citizens' initiative

This innovation was introduced by the Lisbon Treaty. When a sufficient number of citizens share a view — indicated by a minimum of 1 million signatures — the citizens' initiative enables them to invite the Commission to make legislative proposals in fields where the treaty assigns competences to the EU.

Given the unique opportunity that this new instrument offers to bring the Union closer to citizens, and following an extensive public consultation at the start of the year, the Commission proposed rules to set up the instrument so that citizens could start benefiting from this new right as soon as possible.

In December, the European Parliament and the Council reached an agreement on these rules [4] which will make sure that citizens' initiatives are representative of an EU interest while ensuring that the instrument remains easy to use by citizens. Statements of support from citizens have to be collected within one year from the date of registration of the proposed initiative. This new tool should help promote increased cross-border debate about EU policies.

BUILDING A CITIZENS' EUROPE:
JUSTICE, FUNDAMENTAL RIGHTS AND CITIZENSHIP

Justice

On the basis of the Stockholm action plan, the Commission launched an ambitious agenda of justice reforms, covering both civil and criminal law matters.

In civil matters, the Commission proposed a new legal framework for cross-border divorce cases. The new framework (called the Rome III regulation) allows couples from two different EU countries, those living in different countries or living together in a country other than their own to choose with a new degree of legal certainty the law applicable to divorce and legal separation. There are around 16 million such international couples in the EU. As the Rome III regulation was blocked in the Council given that not all Member States were willing to participate, the Commission made, in March, for the first time in the history of the Union, use of the so-called enhanced cooperation procedure. This procedure, put in place by the Treaty of Amsterdam, allows the Commission to move ahead on an issue with a smaller group of Member States under the condition that this enhanced cooperation remains open for all Member States to join. Both the European Parliament and Council agreed to the use of enhanced cooperation in this case and, by the end of the year, 14 Member States had decided to join the new rules for cross-border divorces. This served as a precedent for the later Commission proposal to make use of enhanced cooperation with regard to the Union patent.

In June, the Court of Justice clarified certain rules concerning the recognition and enforcement of judgments requiring the return of a child who has been wrongfully removed. This is an application of the regulation concerning jurisdiction and the recognition and enforcement of judgments in matrimonial matters and matters of parental responsibility [5].

On 1 July, the Commission put the issue of a European contract law high on the agenda, by means of a Green Paper, by establishing an Expert Group on Contract Law and by bringing together a sounding board of business organisations, consumer organisations and legal professionals to discuss this issue. Its aim is, among others, to create a European regime for certain contracts (a so-called '28th regime') which could be chosen by contracting parties for their transactions within the EU's single market. The Commission wants, in particular, small and medium-sized companies to offer their products and services to consumers in other countries without having to become an expert in the national contract law systems of all other 26 Member States. With the Green Paper, the Commission launched a public consultation which was due to end in January 2011. Legislative proposals are planned for later in the year.

In August, the Commission called for saving time and money in cross-border legal disputes through mediation: the potential of existing EU rules on mediation in cross-border legal disputes is effective only if put in place by Member States at national level. Member States have until May 2011 to implement the directive on mediation agreed in 2008.

In December, the Commission proposed new measures for cutting costs and red tape for citizens and businesses in recognising court rulings and civil status documents. The objectives are to eliminate the legal costs (which average €2 000) currently required — usually as a pure formality — to have a legal judgment recognised in another EU country, and to make sure that public documents — such as a contract or deed to a property — circulate without the need for additional procedures. The proposed initiatives will reduce bureaucracy, saving money for businesses and consumers, while reinforcing the single market and making life easier for people living and working in other EU countries. The Commission sought solutions to ease cross-border transactions, with a Green Paper on policy options for progress towards a European contract law for consumers and businesses, and tackled tax obstacles for citizens operating across borders.

In criminal matters, the Commission's priority was to strengthen the rights to a fair trial in the EU. The Commission proposed, in March, new legislation to help people anywhere in the EU when they cannot understand the language of the criminal proceedings they are involved in. This obliges Member States to provide suspects or accused persons with interpretation and translation services for essential documents. The Commission also proposed, in July, legislation on the right to information, basically suggesting an indicative model of a letter of rights listing basic rights of suspects and accused persons during criminal proceedings. As more Europeans travel, study and work outside their home country, assuring such rights across the EU helps build mutual trust between judges and citizens, and fosters the implementation of the principle of mutual recognition of judicial decisions in criminal matters. As a result, the chances are improved for successful application of EU mutual recognition-based measures to fight crime — such as the European Arrest Warrant. The European Parliament and Council agreed to the directive on the right to interpretation and translation in October, and the Council politically endorsed the directive on the right to information in December.

A NEW LEGAL WEBSITE FOR ALL

In July, the Commission launched an e-justice portal [6], which is a focal point for citizens and legal practitioners, designed to ease access to justice and help anyone seeking advice on cross-border legal problems, whether in civil or in criminal matters.

In July, the Commission launched a public consultation on how to improve the rights of victims in criminal proceedings to inform proposals to be made in 2011.

Cooperation between Member States' judicial authorities is key to the effective fight against cross-border crime. Eurojust and the European judicial network in criminal matters have constantly contributed to establishing direct contacts between national judges and to coordinating investigation in cross-border crimes.

Fundamental rights

The Treaty of Lisbon makes the Charter of Fundamental Rights of the European Union (drawn up in 1999–2000 by a Convention) legally binding and gives it the same legal status as the EU treaties. The charter demands respect first of all by the EU institutions when they make laws or decisions. This is why the new College of Commissioners, when taking its oath before the Court of Justice on 3 May 2010, did so not only on the treaties, but also on the charter. In addition, the Commission adopted, in October, a strategy to ensure that all new measures proposed by the Commission or by other institutions will have to be checked against a 'fundamental rights checklist', so that they are compatible with the charter. Furthermore, citizens should be made aware of the circumstances in which they may invoke the charter, which first of all applies to the EU institutions and to the Member States only when they implement EU law. The charter thus complements, but does not replace, national constitutional orders with their own systems of fundamental rights protection.

To complete the system of fundamental rights protection in the EU, the Lisbon Treaty also requires the EU to join the Council of Europe's European Convention for the Protection of Human Rights and Fundamental Freedoms. On 7 July, on the basis of a mandate from the Council, the Commission initiated negotiations with the Council of Europe for this purpose. Ensuring an efficient integration of the Union's legal system of fundamental rights protection into the Council of Europe's system, while preserving the autonomy of the Union's legal order, is the key negotiation objective. Upon successful conclusion of these negotiations by the Council, and ratification by the European Parliament, the 27 EU Member States and the 20 further Member States of the Council of Europe, individuals will be allowed to bring complaints — after they have exhausted domestic remedies — at the European Court of Human Rights in Strasbourg about alleged violations of fundamental rights by the EU. In addition, the EU will have an EU judge representing the Union's own legal order at the European Court of Human Rights.

© European Union

Viviane Reding, Commission Vice-President responsible for justice, fundamental rights and citizenship, at a press conference in September.

Two fundamental rights featured prominently on the EU's agenda throughout the year: privacy and data protection (Articles 7 and 8 of the charter). In November, the Commission set out a strategy on how to protect individuals' data in all policy areas, including law enforcement, while reducing red tape for business and guaranteeing the free circulation of data within the EU. It proposed modernising the EU framework for data protection through strengthening individuals' rights, enhancing the single market dimension, revising data protection rules in the area of police and criminal justice, ensuring high levels of protection for data transferred outside the EU, and more effective enforcement of the rules. The Commission also obtained a mandate from the Council to start negotiations on a personal data protection agreement between the European Union and the United States concerning cooperation to fight terrorism or crime. The aim is to ensure a high level of protection of all types of personal data when transferred and processed for law enforcement purposes as part of transatlantic cooperation.

Equality and non-discrimination continued to play an important role in the EU's fundamental rights agenda in 2010. In January, the Court of Justice confirmed, with regard to a German employment law, the existence of the principle of non-discrimination on grounds of age and the role of national courts in its application [7]. In a later judgment, the Court applied this principle, considering that depriving a worker of a severance allowance because he or she may draw an old age pension constitutes discrimination on grounds of age [8].

In March, the Commission adopted a women's charter to outline the political priority given to the fundamental rights of gender equality in the work of the new Commission. On this basis, the Commission adopted a five-year strategy for promoting gender equality in September. This strategy aims in particular to make better use of women's potential, thereby contributing to the EU's overall economic and social goals. Objectives range from getting more women into supervisory boards of publicly listed companies to tackling gender-based violence.

In November, the Commission presented a 10-year strategy on disability, with the purpose of making Europe more accessible and barrier free. Standardisation and public procurement are key instruments which the Commission will use for this purpose over the next years. The Commission will also explore the feasibility of a European accessibility act.

The challenges of the social and economic integration of Roma — Europe's largest ethnic minority — as well as related free movement issues were of particular concern for the EU in 2010. The Commission had put the issue on the agenda on 7 April with its communication 'The social and economic integration of the Roma in Europe'([9]). Thereafter, the removal of Roma from France in summer 2010 prompted several reactions and interventions from the Commission in August, September and October. The issue was intensely debated at a European Council in September and at the European Parliament. As a result, France as well as other Member States adapted their national legislation to the requirements of the EU's free movement directive of 2004. The Commission set up a Roma task force which has the mandate to analyse to what extent EU and national funds are being effectively used for projects helping the social and economic integration of Roma both in countries of origin and in host countries. First findings of the Roma task force in December show that an EU strategy for a more targeted funding of Roma integration by all Member States is needed. Such a strategy has therefore been included in the Commission's work programme for the first semester of 2011.

© Vadim Ghirda / AP / Reporters

The situation of Roma in their countries of origin as well as in several host countries across the EU hit the headlines in 2010. Here, a group of Roma attend an annual festival in Costesti, Romania.

Following the 2006 communication 'Towards an EU strategy on the rights of the child'([10]), the 116000 hotline was set up for missing children and their parents to call for help wherever they are in the EU. Three years after adoption, the hotline is functioning in 13 Member States. The European Commission adopted in November a communication aiming to offer practical help to the remaining 14 EU countries that have not yet implemented the hotline, while ensuring a high quality of service throughout the EU.

Citizens

In October, the Commission published a 25-point plan to bring concrete benefits to EU citizens on the move. The 'EU citizenship report', adopted on 27 October, aims at enhancing mobility by removing the barriers citizens still face when exercising their right of moving to a Member State other than their own, to study or work, set up a business, start a family or retire. The Court has, in particular, ruled that citizens are entitled to reside in another Member State purely as citizens of the Union ([11]), thus recognising EU citizenship as a source of free movement rights.

The Commission is acting to ensure these rights are fully respected. These rights are equally important when citizens travel, marry, buy or inherit property, vote, receive medical treatment or just shop online from companies established in other Member States.

The proposed 25 concrete measures which the Commission plans to take over the next three years will make life easier for EU citizens when exercising their rights in another EU country. The measures will simplify formalities and conditions for citizens to enjoy their rights. They range from updating rules protecting holidaymakers from bankruptcy of their travel provider during their holiday, to reinforcing the right to consular protection for EU citizens abroad, and from helping consumers get redress if they have problems with a trader, to making it simpler and quicker for people working in another EU country to transfer their social security rights. Car owners will benefit from simplified paperwork for the registration of cars bought in another EU country, and smaller firms from simpler accounting rules.

As to European citizenship, the Court of Justice stated that withdrawal of naturalisation obtained by deception could result in the loss of citizenship of the Union. However, the withdrawal decision would have to respect the principle of proportionality ([12]).

The EU citizenship report identified gaps between rules and reality: citizens still face obstacles in their daily lives, particularly in cross-border situations. The problems frequently encountered include cumbersome administration when registering a car bought in another Member State, complex rules on reimbursement for healthcare obtained in other countries, or difficulties in securing consular services from another Member State when in a country where their home Member State does not have representation.

Citizens getting increasingly mobile between EU countries

Around 12 million European citizens live in a different EU country to that in which they were born. Many more have cross-border experiences when travelling, studying or working, possibly getting married or divorced, buying or inheriting property, voting, receiving medical treatment or just shopping online. There are 16 million marriages with a cross-border dimension. Some 2 million European students have studied in another Member State since the launch of the Erasmus programme. As a result, many are keen to use their rights as European citizens. Too many, however, are still prevented from doing so. It should also be noted that an additional 30 million EU citizens live permanently in a non-EU country, but only in three countries (China, Russia and the United States) are all 27 Member States represented.

HOME AFFAIRS: AN OPEN AND SECURE EUROPE

Policies in this area promote a stable, lawful and secure environment where everyone should feel safe, and where we join forces to address organised and cross-border crime and terrorism — an area without internal borders where EU citizens and non-EU nationals may enter, move, live and work.

A MORE SECURE EUROPEAN UNION

After taking stock in a communication in July of the achievements and challenges in EU counterterrorism policy, the Commission set out an internal security strategy in November. It identifies five priority areas where the EU can bring real added value: serious and organised crime; terrorism; cybercrime; border management; and natural and man-made disasters. The strategy establishes a new joint approach to responding to security threats and challenges. It covers 2011–14, and envisages action based on solid evidence and appreciation of threats and risks, while respecting fundamental rights and protection of personal data.

Security

In order to become effective, the Europe 2020 strategy needs to be deployed in a secure and lawful environment. The Commission has evaluated its tools and instruments to ensure the right balance between security and rights of citizens. It has taken initiatives to increase the security of all EU citizens — notably in preventing terrorism and organised crime.

The European Network and Information Security Agency was also modified to increase European cross-border capability to prevent, detect and better respond to network and information security incidents.

A long-term agreement was negotiated with the USA on the processing and transfer of financial data for the purpose of fighting terrorism (the TFTP agreement — see box), and entered into force in August. A proposal for a regulation laying down common rules to limit access to some chemicals that can be misused as precursors to produce home-made explosives was tabled in September.

The EU–US Terrorist Finance Tracking Programme

This agreement on the transfer of financial messaging data from Europe allows targeted searches for counterterrorism investigations under the US Terrorist Finance Tracking Programme (TFTP). It was reached after difficult negotiations to ensure an adequate level of protection of Europeans' data. Under the terms of the agreement [13], Europol verifies all US requests before any data is transferred and an independent EU scrutiniser is posted in Washington to monitor compliance with the agreement's strict requirements whenever US officials look at this information. The functioning will be regularly reviewed, starting in February 2011, and the Commission will report on the outcome to the European Parliament and Council. The Commission started work in November on the creation of an equivalent European system, which will eventually allow extraction of data on EU soil, thus ending the transfer of bulk data to the USA.

In the fight against terrorism, the Court of Justice specified the scope of the Council regulation. It imposed the freezing of funds and other economic resources of persons associated with Usama bin Laden, the Al-Qaeda network or the Taliban [14]. It notably stated that the freezing of funds does not apply to certain social security benefits paid to their spouses [15].

It also stated that the Council decisions which included the DHKP-C (the Revolutionary People's Liberation Party-Front in Turkey) on lists relating to measures for combating terrorism before June 2007, adopted in breach of basic procedural safeguards, cannot form any part of the basis for criminal proceedings against members of that organisation who are not on those lists [16].

The General Court annulled certain Council measures ordering the freezing of funds of Stichting Al-Aqsa with a view to combating terrorism ([17]).

A communication adopted in July on information exchange in the area of justice, freedom and security set out the principles underpinning the development of future internal security initiatives. It also proposed a European Information Exchange Model, to bring clarity to European citizens concerned about data sharing by public authorities.

A communication on a strategy for transferring passenger name records (PNR) to other countries was approved in September. PNR data have proven to be an important tool in the fight against serious transnational crime and terrorism but, at the same time, they raise important issues about protection of personal data. The Commission communication focused on protecting passengers' personal data and the mechanics of data transfer. It also stressed the importance of sharing analytical information obtained from PNR with police and judicial authorities within the EU, as a contribution to European citizens' security. The communication was accompanied by three negotiation mandates for agreements with Australia, Canada and the USA, which were adopted by the Council in December.

The use of airport body scanners was assessed, and the Commission urged common standards for their operation as well as full respect of fundamental rights (notably human dignity and privacy) if Member States opt to deploy them. In response to new threats to civil aviation, an ad hoc High-Level Working Group co-chaired by the Commission and the Belgian Presidency explored possible enhancements of security systems for cargo and mail. This was done in close cooperation with Member States and operators, based on common threat and risk assessments and better integration with intelligence. This group's report with recommendations for further actions was endorsed by the Council in December.

Steps were taken towards a stronger legal framework with tougher penalties to counter trafficking in human beings and child sexual abuse, sexual exploitation and child pornography. Following proposals from the Commission adopted in March, the European Parliament and Council agreed on the text of a directive on the fight against trafficking in human beings, including minimum rules concerning the definition of criminal offences, the level of sanctions and protection of victims [18]. Once adopted, the new rules will strengthen crime prevention and the protection of victims of trafficking. Moreover, in December, the Commission appointed a European anti-trafficking coordinator who will have a central role in coordinating all aspects of policies against this crime. The coordinator will also help elaborate existing and new EU policies relevant to the fight against trafficking and provide overall strategic policy orientation for the EU's external policy in this field. Finally, the Commission launched a new website [19] dedicated to the fight against trafficking in human beings. This website should become a one-stop shop at EU level for practitioners and the public interested in knowing more about trafficking and how it is being addressed within the EU.

Stricter rules were proposed in May to protect European citizens from attacks against information systems and cybercrime. Under the proposed rules, the perpetrators of cyber attacks and the producers of related and malicious software could be prosecuted, and would face heavier criminal sanctions. Member States would also be obliged to quickly respond to urgent requests for help in the case of cyber attacks, rendering European justice and police cooperation in this area more effective. Europol, the European Police Office, became an EU agency at the start of the year. The Commission initiated a reflection on its future regime under the Treaty of Lisbon, backed up with a December communication on the procedures for democratic scrutiny over Europol's activities, paving the way for a more robust parliamentary control system over them. The communication supports the idea of creating a joint body through which the European Parliament and national parliaments can exercise control over Europol. It also proposes ways to increase transparency in Europol's work.

Openness

The European Union is constantly seeking the right balance between maintaining secure borders and remaining open to legitimate access by people from other countries — a balance which is forged in its policies on migration, visas and asylum.

In the area of migration, the goal is a policy which — as foreseen in the Europe 2020 strategy — clears the way for legal immigration, which is an asset for a sustainable economic recovery and, at the same time, addresses illegal migration. Priority is being given to consolidating a genuine common immigration and asylum policy. It includes new and flexible admission systems for labour immigration and initiatives to support integration of immigrants. It aims for progress in building a common European asylum system based on solidarity and the respect for fundamental rights.

The EU is building a Europe that is open and secure at the same time. Here, a cybercrime police unit in Lille monitors the Internet to track down fraudulent use, scams and identity theft.

In line with the Lisbon Treaty's new legal base for support measures for the integration of legally residing non-EU nationals, the Council in June endorsed support for Member States' policies through knowledge exchange and improved coordination. It announced a new European agenda on integration. The EU is moving towards a new and flexible admission system for economic immigration.

In July, a proposal on seasonal workers from beyond the EU was made to establish a simple and fast-track common EU-wide admissions system. The aim is to protect this particularly vulnerable group with a secure legal status to prevent exploitation and to protect health and safety. At the same time, a proposal on intra-corporate transferees aimed to make it easier for multinational companies to temporarily transfer non-EU skilled workers into branches or subsidiaries within the EU. In May, a four-year action plan was proposed on unaccompanied minors. It covers prevention, regional protection, reception and identification of durable solutions. It takes account of the interests of the child and the Charter of Fundamental Rights as well as the UN Convention on the Rights of the Child. The Council endorsed the approach in June.

New requirements — and a budget — were agreed for completing the Schengen Information System. This system aims to ensure a high level of control and security at the Union's external borders, as well as to assist cooperation on law enforcement. The Visa Information System for the exchange of visa data among Member States also progressed, and from 2011 onwards will help in implementing the Schengen common visa policy, as well as preventing terrorism and other internal security threats.

Work on a common European asylum system continued. It involved the formal establishment of the European Asylum Support Office in Malta in November, and further negotiations on modified legislation as well as a joint resettlement scheme. The European Asylum Support Office will enhance solidarity among Member States and help them in fulfilling their European and international obligations in this field. It will develop practical cooperation among Member States on asylum, by facilitating exchange of information on countries of origin, by providing them with support for translation and interpretation, training of asylum officials and assisting in the relocation of recognised refugees. It will also support Member States under 'particular pressure', in particular through the establishment of an early warning system, and coordinating teams of experts to assist EU countries in managing asylum applications and in putting in place appropriate reception facilities. Finally, it will collect and enhance the exchange of information on best practices, drawing up an annual report on the asylum situation in the EU and adopting technical documents, such as guidelines and operating manuals.

The EU aims to ensure a high level of control and security at its external borders. Border guards — such as here on the Bulgarian–Turkish border — use sophisticated equipment and intelligence to prevent illegal traffic.

A modified legal framework was proposed for the border operations coordination agency, Frontex, to strengthen its operational capabilities and to reinforce consideration of fundamental rights (with particular emphasis on return operations). New rules on sea border and rescue operations were agreed to ensure that measures taken in the context of sea border surveillance operations coordinated by Frontex fully respect fundamental rights and non-refoulement — the principle of international law that protects refugees from being returned to places where their lives or freedoms could be threatened.

Frontex Rapid Border Intervention Teams were activated for the first time when Greece requested operational assistance in responding to urgent and exceptional pressure at points along its external borders in October, as large numbers of non-EU nationals tried to enter illegally.

The European Parliament and Council agreed on the necessary amendments to a 2003 directive which governs the status of non-EU nationals who are long-term residents, refugees and beneficiaries of subsidiary protection but not currently entitled to long-term resident status. With these amendments, refugees and beneficiaries of subsidiary protection will be able to acquire long-term resident status in the Member States of the EU on a similar basis to other non-EU nationals who have lived legally in the EU for more than five years. The new rules will enable beneficiaries of international protection who become long-term residents to take up residence in a Member State other than that in which they are recognised. Under certain conditions, they would enjoy equality of treatment with citizens of the EU Member State in which they reside in a wide range of economic and social areas, including education and access to the labour market and social security benefits. Furthermore, the new rules also strengthen safeguards against refoulement (expulsion).

The Court of Justice stipulated the circumstances under which a person could lose refugee status. In June, it also specified the conditions in which an application for refugee status made by a displaced Palestinian in a Member State must be examined [20].

Close analysis of national conditions in Albania and Bosnia and Herzegovina led to a decision to lift the short-stay visa obligation on citizens of these two countries. The Visa Code which became applicable in April harmonised procedures and enhanced transparency for the more than 10 million people who apply for Schengen visas every year. Good progress was recorded towards full visa reciprocity with non-EU countries, including visa waiver agreements with Brazil and Schengen visa-free status for Taiwan.

INVOLVING CITIZENS AND EASING EVERYDAY CONCERNS

Citizens have obtained new benefits across a wide range of the activities where the EU has influence. They enjoy increasing opportunities for access to and involvement in the way the EU operates. From cheaper mobile phone calls to easier switching between energy providers or better protection while travelling, and from safer products to healthier food, the EU has maintained and continually developed its interventions on behalf of citizens. Competition policy has helped create market dynamics that are favourable to consumers, the rights of workers and spouses have been enhanced by social policy, and responses to fires and flood damage have been upgraded by legislation, cooperation and coordination at EU level.

SERVICES

Telecoms

Mobile phone users benefited from further EU-imposed price cuts and guarantees (see box), and more are under consideration: the Commission concluded in June that competition is still not providing sufficient choice to consumers. A revised telecom regulatory framework included the establishment of the Body of European Regulators for Electronic Communications. This will improve the consistency of the EU regulatory framework for telecoms, thereby improving conditions for citizens as consumers.

A COMMON CHARGER FOR MOBILE PHONES

Mobile phones are fine — until the battery goes flat and you do not have your charger with you. No calls. No access to your data or your contacts. Then a frantic search for a compatible charger starts. But that will soon be a problem of the past. Thanks to pressure from the Commission, 13 of the leading phone makers have agreed on a harmonised system for data-enabled phones sold in the EU. All these phones can be charged with a simple micro-USB plug. The result for the environment is less electrical waste. Common sense, rather than new legislation, has led to this achievement.

Lower roaming tariffs in the EU protect consumers from bill-shocks.

Roaming — a big win for citizens

From 1 July 2010, new caps on travellers' data-roaming limits came into effect. In addition, maximum wholesale prices for data roaming have fallen from €1 to 80 cent per megabyte. The maximum price for making a roaming call has been cut to 39 cent per minute (excluding VAT), from the pre-July 2010 cost of 43 cent, while receiving a call will cost a maximum of 15 cent per minute (excluding VAT), instead of 19 cent. Since 2005, costs have been cut by as much as 70 % for citizens making calls on their mobile phones while in another Member State. A text message between EU Member States costs 60 % less than it did in 2005. On 8 December, the European Commission launched a public consultation to seek the views of consumers, businesses, telecom operators and public authorities on the EU mobile phone roaming market.

In June, the Court of Justice confirmed the validity of the so-called roaming regulation ([21]). It lays down maximum charges for calls made and received by users outside their own network ([22]).

Financial services

Beyond the repair work to the financial sector (see Chapter 1), the interests of the citizen were directly addressed. In March, the Commission promoted dialogue with banking and consumer associations on transparency on bank fees (which led to the launch of an industry-led bank fees initiative in November). This was designed to lead to a code of conduct. A new section on financial literacy was launched in April on Dolceta, the online consumer education tool, covering spending, saving and investing, borrowing, and protecting or insuring.

The Commission sponsored online consumer education on financial literacy in April and May and, in July, set up a Financial Services User Group to strengthen the representation of consumers, retail investors and other users of financial services at EU level. This group is also to advise the Commission on issues affecting users of financial services such as retail banking, mortgage credit and insurance. The Commission sought solutions to ease cross-border transactions, with a Green Paper on policy options for progress towards a European contract law for consumers and businesses, and tackled tax obstacles for citizens operating across borders.

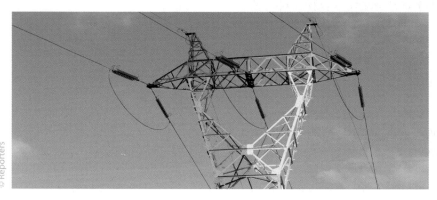

The electricity market has been reviewed in order to enable consumers to avail themselves of better tools to assess prices and services. Here, an electricity pylon carrying high-voltage lines.

Energy

The Commission reviewed how electricity markets are performing for retail consumers. The aim is to enable consumers to exercise choice in the market place, by giving them tools to assess prices and services. Working with consumers, regulators and industry, the Commission also put forward recommendations for making energy bills clear, concise and comparable.

Services and services of general interest

Services of general interest also fall within the scope of EU rules. Guidance was updated at the end of October on the application of state aid, public procurement and internal market rules to services of general economic interest and, in particular, to social services of general interest. At the same time, the Commission published its second biennial report on social services of general interest.

In June, the Commission consulted on the implementation process for the services directive, which came into effect at the end of December 2009.

HEALTH AND CONSUMERS

The Commission reinforced its capacity to determine where the single market was not working for consumers. It identified continuing problems in cross-border e-commerce and in national enforcement regimes for consumer protection. It also pinpointed the main consumer markets underperforming for consumers. It highlighted obstacles in the retail electricity market to effective consumer choice and switching providers. Performance was reviewed for the European Consumer Centres network, which handles 60 000 complaints per year, and a mid-term evaluation of the consumer policy strategy 2007–13 was concluded. This will feed into the design of the strategy post-2013.

In the area of retail financial services, a dialogue between banking and consumer associations on transparency and comparability led to the formal launch of an industry-led bank fees initiative in November. This was designed to lead to a code of conduct.

In January, the Court of Justice stated that allowing customers to take part in a lottery free of charge following a certain number of purchases can, in certain specific circumstances, constitute an unfair commercial practice, prohibited by the European unfair commercial practices directive. In the context of a preliminary ruling concerning the directive on the protection of consumers in respect of distance contracts [23], the Court ruled that consumers should not be charged delivery costs if they withdraw from a distance contract. In such a case, only the cost of returning the goods may be charged to the consumer [24].

Product safety

Product safety was kept under review with impact assessments and consultations on the 2001 general product safety directive and the 1987 directive on food imitating products. New requirements were also considered for bathing articles for children and for childproof locking devices for windows and balcony doors [25]. International cooperation led to a trilateral meeting with the Chinese and US authorities. New guidelines for the EU's rapid information system on hazardous products came into effect in January, clarifying procedures and tightening up risk assessment. Action was maintained against hazards from materials and products as diverse as dimethylfumarate and novelty cigarette lighters. Rules for plastic materials in contact with food were updated.

Food safety

EU measures to control BSE (the so-called 'mad cow' disease) — including the minimum age limit for testing cattle for the disease — were further reviewed. An initiative to review meat inspections systems was launched with scientific input from the European Food Safety Authority (EFSA) on criteria and methodology. In November, more than €250 million was earmarked to support programmes to eradicate, control and monitor animal diseases in 2011. New limits were set and new checks were run on contaminants and residues of veterinary drugs and pesticides. New approvals were given to active substances included in plant protection products, and new obligations were imposed on manufacturers. The list of currently authorised food additives was reviewed, and the first EU list for approved flavourings was created — for smoke flavours. Controls were tightened up on imports of certain feed and food of non-animal origin.

In October, the European Parliament reiterated its commitment to preventing the sale of meat and milk from cloned animals in the EU. This followed the Commission's publication of a report on cloning which advocates a five-year moratorium on the sale of food from cloned animals and on the use of cloning for food production purposes. The European Parliament and Council are set to enter into conciliation negotiations to try and find an agreement on proposed updates to 'novel foods' rules.

Reflecting the central importance of food quality for every farmer and consumer, the Commission adopted a string of proposals in December. These encourage diversification of agricultural production, ensure fair competition and help farmers to communicate better the qualities of their products. This so-called 'quality package' makes it easier for consumers to use and understand EU quality schemes, such as the 'protected designation of origin, protected geographical indication' and 'traditional speciality guaranteed'. These measures also help improve voluntary certification schemes for agricultural products and foodstuffs through best practice guidelines.

The Commission has improved food labelling. It has worked in collaboration with the European Parliament and Council to advance the 'food information to consumers' proposal, to enable consumers to make informed choices, taking into account nutrition and dietary advice. New EU rules on organic food labelling, including the requirement to display the new EU organic logo, entered into force in July. From the start of the year, food in the EU became safer thanks to more controls and fewer and less harmful residues — owing in part to the withdrawal from the market of harmful pesticides, and in part to the strengthening of the Union's border control activity.

To protect citizens against misleading health claims on food, the Commission is working to establish lists of permitted health claims, based on the scientific assessment of EFSA and following authorisation procedures at EU level. In 2010, three health claims were authorised and 15 were rejected. At the end of the process, only substantiated health claims will be permitted on the EU market. Initiatives (non-regulatory) are also under way to encourage stakeholders to continue efforts in the reformulation of food products with respect to nutrients that may increase the risk of chronic diseases.

© BSIP / Reporters

The EU has improved food labelling to enable consumers to make informed choices. The new compulsory EU organic logo entered into force in July.

Genetically modified foods

In July, the Commission adopted a proposal setting out a new flexible approach on GMO cultivation, which takes into consideration Member State desires, but also retains the basis of solid science for any GMO authorisation. According to this proposal, cultivation decisions lie with Member States, while authorisation decisions remain at EU level. In November, the Commission services finalised a draft regulation referred to as a 'technical solution for the low-level presence of non-authorised GM material in feed' or 'LLP'. This proposal will provide legal certainty to feed operators importing feed material from third countries by harmonising official control of GMOs for which an application is pending in the EU, or for which an EU authorisation has expired.

The Commission also prepared a report on the socioeconomic implications of GMO cultivation, based on contributions from 24 Member States. The development of guidelines for the environmental risk assessment of GMOs was based on an update to the EFSA guidance published in November. External evaluations of GMO legislation as regards cultivation and food and feed have been carried out. These may be followed by an impact analysis of possible policy changes by mid-2012. The Commission adopted a decision authorising a GM potato for cultivation. Other decisions on food and feed uses are still under examination. The guidelines for the risk assessment of GM food and feed are being finalised after consultations with Member States, EFSA and stakeholders.

Medical products and services

As to free circulation of medical services in the internal market, the Court of Justice judged that public authorities may offer financial incentives to induce doctors to prescribe cheaper medicinal products, provided notably that the incentive scheme is based on non-discriminatory objective criteria [26]. The Court also specified the conditions in which demographic and geographical limits can be set by the competent authorities of a Member State for the opening of new pharmacies, in order to ensure adequate pharmaceutical services [27]. And it ruled that where unscheduled hospital care is administered during a temporary stay in a Member State other than the Member State of affiliation, the latter is not required to reimburse the patient as regards costs which, in the State where the care was administered, fall to the patient to pay [28].

Quality and safety of substances of human origin for medical use

On tissues and cells of human origin, the EU has advanced towards a consistent level of competence and performance of inspections and control measures, with new guidelines on the training and qualification of officials. In July, new rules were adopted on standards of quality and safety of human organs intended for transplantation, covering procurement and transplantation activities, traceability, reporting of adverse reactions and safe transportation.

Action against counterfeiting

EU customs authorities seized large quantities of drug precursors — legitimate goods used by the perfume industry but illicitly deviated for the manufacture of synthetic drugs such as ecstasy — including 240 tonnes of acetic anhydride, the main heroin precursor. They also intercepted 118 million fake products, including many presenting potential danger to citizens — from cigarettes to shampoos, and medicines to household appliances.

Action against smoking

The Commission launched a public consultation with a view to reviewing the 2001 rules on tobacco products to respond to health risks and to overcome persistent differences between Member States' provisions on manufacture, presentation and sale of tobacco products. The phasing out of direct subsidies for tobacco also began this year.

CLASSIFYING PLANTS

The Commission registered some 2 800 new plant varieties in the common catalogues. Currently, therefore, around 19 700 varieties of agricultural crops and 17 300 varieties of vegetable crops can be marketed throughout the EU. The Commission finalised the 'conservation material' package of legislation on less stringent requirements for marketing of seed for the purposes of conservation of genetic resources and natural environment.

In 2010, the applications for protection of plant variety intellectual rights increased slightly, with some 17 500 plant varieties currently protected. In order to solve issues related to farm use of protected plant varieties, a stakeholders' working group developed ideas for future solutions.

© AFP / Belga

Polish customs officers inspect a car filled with cigarettes on the border with Kaliningrad Oblast, Russia. EU customs and tax officials fight smuggling that can undermine its citizens' health as well as the EU's excise revenues.

BENEFITING FROM A FAIR MARKET

Citizens have benefited from the operation of EU competition policy. The Commission has vigorously enforced competition rules, through its actions to combat cartels and other anticompetitive practices, as well through its merger control activity. In particular, the Commission has agreed sanctions against a number of large cartels, which are the most harmful type of competition law infringement.

Tackling anticompetitive behaviour

In 2010, the Commission fined 17 bathroom equipment manufacturers €622 million for coordinating price increases for baths, sinks and taps for 12 years in six countries covering 240 million people. Not only will this cartel have harmed businesses in the construction and plumbing sectors, but a large number of consumers will also have been affected. Eleven air cargo carriers were also fined a total of €799 million for coordinating surcharges for fuel and security over a six-year period. Such collusive behaviour harms European businesses and consumers. In June, the Commission fined 17 producers of prestressing steel a total of €458 million for operating a price-fixing and market-sharing cartel between 1984 and 2002. The infringement covered all but three of the then Member States and therefore was of importance for nearly the entire European construction market. In December, the Commission fined six producers of liquid crystal display (LCD) panels a total of €648 million for operating a cartel which harmed European buyers of television sets, computer monitors and electronic notebooks, a key component of which is a LCD panel. Exposing and putting a stop to such cartels gives competitors and customers the chance to innovate and grow. It also provides consumers with wider choice, better quality and more competitive prices.

Besides cartels, the Commission fined the professional association of pharmacists in France €5 million for opposing forms of group structuring that would allow foreign companies operating in the sector of laboratory analysis to reduce costs, improve the quality of tests and ultimately compete effectively with those already established in France. Prices of clinical laboratory tests in France are some of the highest in the EU. In the decision, the Commission invoked for the first time a rule whereby members of an association of undertakings that has infringed competition law may be held liable if the association itself has insufficient funds to pay the fine.

In 2010, the Court of Justice and the General Court both issued several rulings in the field of competition law.

The Court of Justice confirmed a judgment of the General Court stating that internal company communications with in-house lawyers are not covered by legal professional privilege, having regard to in-house lawyers' economic dependence and the close ties that they have with their employers, as well as the fact that they do not enjoy the same level of professional independence as external lawyers [29].

Moreover, the Court of Justice decided on the extent to which the Commission is bound by the principle of proportionality when accepting commitments offered by undertakings which are being investigated under Articles 101 and 102 TFEU. It also gave guidance on the procedural rights enjoyed by third party undertakings directly affected in their interests by these 'commitment decisions' adopted pursuant to Article 9 of Regulation (EC) No 1/2003 [30]. In the same way, the General Court confirmed that the Commission enjoys a margin of discretion when fixing the level of the fines imposed in the case of an infringement of the competition rules [31].

In addition, the Court of Justice upheld the €12.6 million fine imposed on Deutsche Telekom for abuse of its dominant position in the fixed telephony markets in Germany [32].

In July, the General Court essentially upheld the decision of the Commission finding that AstraZeneca abused its dominant position by preventing the marketing of generic products replicating their anti-ulcer product, Losec. The Court slightly reduced the fine payable by AstraZeneca to €52.5 million [33].

The General Court also upheld the validity of the prohibition of Ryanair's takeover of Aer Lingus [34] and the lawfulness of the Commission decision of 7 January 2004 authorising, subject to the sale of assets, the purchase of Vivendi Universal Publishing by Lagardère.

The Commission has also paid particular attention to fostering competition in key sectors of the economy. Notable examples include the air transport sector, where the Commission expressed concerns that a planned joint venture between British Airways, American Airlines and Iberia may be in breach of EU antitrust rules and may harm consumers. In response to these concerns, the companies provided commitments that will facilitate the entry and expansion of competitors on key transatlantic air routes. The commitments will ensure competition on these routes, resulting in an adequate choice of flights, quality of service and ticket price for consumers. This will also allow the airlines to put in place the transatlantic alliance that they have long aspired to. In the same field, the Commission also approved the British Airways–Iberia merger on the grounds that it will lead to a stronger European air transport industry without harming competition.

In four cases against leading energy companies in Germany, France, Italy and Sweden, the Commission opened up energy markets to more competition, with positive effects on more than 100 million customers (see Chapter 3).

In February, Microsoft started to distribute a browser choice screen to its Windows users, offering them an unbiased choice between web browsers, in line with a decision taken by the Commission in 2009. As a consequence, there is now more choice and competition in the browser market.

The Commission also undertook an in-depth investigation of the planned acquisition by Unilever of the Sara Lee body and laundry care business with a view to ensuring that the merger would not lead to increased prices for consumers. To obtain the Commission's approval of the acquisition, Unilever committed to divesting Sara Lee's Sanex brand and related business in Europe. This clear and workable remedy was deemed sufficient to restore competition to all markets where the Commission had concerns.

In the financial sector, the Commission has accepted commitments offered by Visa Europe to cut significantly its multilateral interchange fees (MIFs) for debit card payments. The MIF is a bank-to-bank fee for card payments that is collectively fixed by Visa Europe's member banks, but is ultimately paid by consumers. Visa Europe also committed to maintain and further develop measures which will increase transparency and competition in the payment cards markets. Lower interbank fees will trigger real benefits for merchants and consumers whilst more transparent rules will also improve competition in the card markets.

SOCIAL RIGHTS

Parental rights

In July, the Court of Justice ruled that workers given leave from work or transferred to another job because of pregnancy are entitled to their basic monthly pay and the supplementary allowances and supplements attached to their occupational status. It also stated that employed fathers are entitled to parental leave, irrespective of the professional status of their child's mother [35].

The European Commission said it would work on a balanced compromise to advance mothers' rights, following a European Parliament vote in October to increase the minimum period of maternity leave to full pay for 20 weeks — more than the 14 to 18 weeks proposed by the Commission.

A directive proposed by the Commission to improve the social protection of self-employed workers and remove disincentives to female entrepreneurship was agreed by the European Parliament in May and the Council in June. The new directive, which entered into force on 4 August, ensures that self-employed women, assisting spouses and life partners of self-employed workers are granted a sufficient maternity allowance and a leave period of at least 14 weeks should they choose to take it. This is the first time a maternity allowance has been granted to self-employed workers at EU level. Assistant spouses and life partners of self-employed workers will have the right to social security coverage (i.e. such as pensions) on an equal basis to that of formal self-employed workers, if the Member State offers such protection. This will help provide a stronger social safety net and prevent women from falling into poverty. Member States may decide whether the maternity allowance and social protection rights are granted on a mandatory or voluntary basis, i.e. upon request. Member States have two years to introduce the legislation into their national laws.

Workers' rights

Workers received further protection when, in March, the EU employment and social affairs ministers adopted a directive to prevent injuries and infections to healthcare workers from sharp objects such as needle sticks — one of the most serious health and safety threats in European workplaces and estimated to cause 1 million injuries each year.

EU research programmes are helping citizens by devising solutions to social issues in Europe. Two issues were examined in major EU conferences in 2010 — different types of inequalities and their role in poverty in Europe, and religion and tolerance and their impact on European cohesion.

The Commission issued a Green Paper in July launching discussions on the future of pensions in the face of demographic change. The aim of the paper is to ensure that the EU puts the right measures in place to support Member States in their difficult task of providing their citizens with adequate, sustainable and safe pensions — both now and in the future. The design of pension systems is largely the responsibility of Member States, but the regulatory framework at EU level covers some important aspects, such as cross-border coordination of social security pensions, the internal market for funded occupational schemes and standards on prudential rules, guarantees in case of the insolvency of enterprises and anti-discrimination. In November, EU ministers approved a report on the subject [36].

Mobility

In May, new rules came into force on social security coordination, aimed at making life easier for Europeans on the move — whether for work or as pensioners, job seekers or tourists. The result is stronger guarantees that rights in the area of sickness insurance, pensions, unemployment and family benefits are preserved when moving within Europe. Information must be provided actively and delivered rapidly by the social security institutions in Member States. More up-to-date procedures will lead to quicker and simpler services for citizens, cutting red tape and reducing the administrative burden for public services, including through a new information network for exchange of social security information and faster access to more benefits for more people.

Inclusivity

The year 2010 was the European Year for Combating Poverty and Social Exclusion. Launched in Madrid in January, the initiative aimed to raise awareness of poverty in Europe, its causes and potential solutions. It included a series of headline events at EU level and over 1 000 projects at national level. The European Parliament adopted a report 'on the role of minimum income in combating poverty and promoting an inclusive society in Europe' in June. A European Platform against Poverty and Social Exclusion was also launched.

The Europe 2020 initiative on poverty reduction (see Chapter 1) sets out how to ensure that the benefits of growth and jobs are widely shared so that those experiencing poverty can take an active part in society. It will notably build on the lessons of the European Year for Combating Poverty and Social Exclusion. In June, employment and social affairs ministers agreed to set a target of lifting at least 20 million out of poverty or exclusion over the next 10 years.

Other achievements on societal issues included an April report on EU funding for the integration of Roma, and the launch of the high-level Roma task force in September to improve how EU funds are spent to help them. There was also dialogue with churches, religious communities and philosophical non-confessional organisations.

Ethics

Reflection was pursued on ethics in science and new technologies in the European group of the same name. In March, the group adopted a five-year report on its activities, summarising the issues covered by its opinions, the role of ethics in the EU policy frame following the adoption of the Lisbon Treaty and the issues that deserve further analysis at EU level. Also in March, the EC International Dialogue on Bioethics took place, with Member States, representatives of the European Parliament, international organisations including the Council of Europe, the World Health Organisation (WHO) and Unesco, and non-EU countries, including Argentina, Australia, Brazil, Canada, China, Egypt, India, Indonesia, Japan, Mexico, the Philippines, Russia, South Africa and the United States.

In parallel, the Commission published newsletters on bioethics and reports on the group's meetings and activities, and set up a web portal on ethics. The EC Inter-service Group on Ethics and EU Policies met three times, to discuss synthetic biology, biosecurity, biotechnology and ICT.

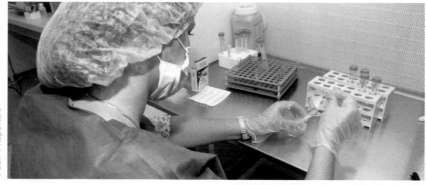

© BSIP / Reporters

Ethics remain at the heart of scientific and technological progress in the EU.

EDUCATION AND CULTURE

In March, ministers from 46 European countries launched the European higher education area, under the Bologna process. It aims to make European higher education more compatible, comparable, competitive and attractive.

In April, the Court of Justice stated that European Union law precludes, in principle, a limitation on enrolment by non-resident students in certain university courses in the public health field, except when such a limitation is proved to be justified with regard to the protection of public health ([37]).

The Commission proposed a European heritage label ([38]) to celebrate and symbolise European integration, ideals and history. In September, it published a communication on support for the digitalisation of European cinema. It also published a report in July on the implementation of the European agenda for culture, and a recommendation on mobility for artists. The Council adopted conclusions on European film heritage ([39]), including the challenges of the digital era, covering the transition from analogue to digital and the link between film funding policies and film heritage.

In November, the Commission assessed the new provisions on sport in the Treaty of Lisbon. The Commission is already promoting social inclusion and other objectives through sport with funding from EU programmes and Structural Funds. For instance, it supports 30 European networks involving 250 partner organisations to promote sport for health, education and training, sport for the disabled, gender equality, the fight against doping and volunteering.

The opening event of 'Ruhr 2010', 'Engel über Zollverein', in Essen, Germany, one of the European Union's Capitals of Culture for 2010.

In the year of the 25th anniversary of the European Capitals of Culture, Pécs (Hungary), Essen for the Ruhr (Germany) and Istanbul (Turkey) were the chosen cities in 2010. The Council designated Umeå (Sweden) and Riga (Latvia) as capitals for 2014 and Mons (Belgium) for 2015, alongside a Czech city still to be formally designated.

Parliament awarded this year's LUX Cinema Prize to *Die Fremde*, by Feo Aladağ of Germany, the first woman ever to compete for the prize. The film highlights the problem of 'honour killings' by depicting the drama of a Turkish family living in Germany. The two other shortlisted finalists were *Akadimia Platonos* by Filippos Tsitos (Greece and Germany) and *Illégal* by Olivier Masset-Depasse (Belgium).

An array of EU prizes awarded in the field of culture

These prizes include the European Border Breakers Awards (for contemporary music) in January, the European Talent Prize (for film writing) in May, the Prize for Cultural Heritage/Europa Nostra Awards in June and the Prize for Literature in November, which went to 11 new and emerging authors selected by national juries from 11 countries (Belgium, Cyprus, Denmark, Estonia, Finland, Germany, Luxembourg, Romania, Slovenia, Spain and the former Yugoslav Republic of Macedonia). Europe's digital library, Europeana, now gives online access to over 14 million examples of Europe's cultural heritage — books, maps, photographs, paintings, film and music clips — to anyone in the world; launched in 2008 with 2 million objects, it has greatly exceeded the initial target for 2010 of 10 million objects. Three films co-funded by the European Union's MEDIA programme were among those honoured at the closing ceremony of the International Rome Film Festival on 5 November.

Figures released in June showed that almost 200 000 higher education students benefited from the Erasmus programme of student exchanges in the 2008/09 academic year — bringing the total beneficiaries since the scheme started in 1987 to over 2 million.

© Franz-Peter Tschauner / Belga

The EU's civil protection mechanism was called into action to help protect parts of Hungary when toxic red mud leaked from an industrial dam.

CIVIL PROTECTION

The EU's civil protection mechanism for crisis and disaster management was brought into play to cope with floods in the spring in Poland, the Czech Republic and Germany. In May, Poland requested the activation of the mechanism and, in response, 14 teams with high-capacity pumps from other Member States and one EU-financed pump run by the three Baltic States helped lower water levels. In light of a growing incidence of natural disasters, the EU reflected on how to reinforce its disaster response capacity, and stepped up the analytical and coordination capacity of its monitoring and information centre. The new internal security strategy aims to bring the new joint approach to bear on natural disasters too — whether earthquakes or forest fires, flooding or severe snowfalls, or crises precipitated by terrorist or cyber attacks on critical infrastructure, energy shortages, health pandemics, major ICT breakdowns or industrial accidents.

PASSENGERS' RIGHTS AND TRANSPORT

Moving around easily — and safely — is important for EU citizens, as is being able to transport the goods and services that they want.

To evaluate whether further measures may be necessary, the Commission reviewed how air carriers apply EU law and how national authorities ensure the enforcement of air passenger rights. In December, a new regulation for passenger rights in maritime and inland waterway transport was adopted and a general agreement was reached on another regulation for bus and coach passengers. This was achieved in conciliation between the Parliament and Council. An information campaign to raise citizens' awareness of their rights as passengers in both air and rail transport was launched during the summer in response to the findings of the *Eurobarometer* of 2009, which identified room for improvement on passenger awareness.

Air

On air passenger rights, the Court of Justice confirmed that the liability of air carriers for destruction, loss, damage or delay of baggage, which is governed by the Montreal Convention[40], is limited to €1 134, including both material and non-material damages[41].

In the air, in addition to action to ease travel in the aftermath of the Icelandic volcano eruption, safe and secure travel was reinforced through regular updating of the list of banned airlines. A June stakeholder hearing was held on air passenger rights. Major steps were made towards a single European sky, which will cut costs and delays for European passengers, and at the same time help to reduce emissions. Future challenges for aviation in Europe were discussed at the first-ever meeting of the Aviation Platform in October, set up to give strategic advice on the basis for a sustainable future for air transport and a competitive future for the European aviation industry.

A European action plan to strengthen air cargo security was agreed in December following proposals by the Commission, after the discovery of explosive devices in air cargo originating in Yemen. The action plan will allow a joint EU approach to the emergency security measures put in place by several Member States to address the new threat to civil aviation.

© Francisco Seco / AP / Reporters

EU legislation has given passengers faced with delays in its territory strengthened rights to food, accommodation and compensation when carriers — in the air, by bus or by rail — are at fault.

Road

Efforts were stepped up on road safety (on top of the 40 % reduction in road fatalities achieved in Europe in recent years), and on increasing road security (with a recommendation on eCall). The Commission adopted ambitious plans to halve the number of road deaths in Europe by 2020 starting in 2010. These plans build on the results of the road safety action programme 2001–10, which has been credited with saving 78 000 lives. In December, the Council reached political agreement on cross-border exchange of information on a number of traffic offences that jeopardise road safety. This directive aims to enable identification of drivers who commit offences in a Member State other than that where their vehicle is registered. Sanctions can therefore be enforced across borders.

Citizens also stand to benefit — through cleaner air and the opportunity to drive quieter and more fuel-efficient vehicles — from EU policies with a strong entrepreneurial character. The EU's green cars initiative is fostering Europe's leadership in clean and energy-efficient vehicle technologies, while in April the Commission presented a new action plan covering continued vehicle emission reductions, support for research and innovation and for common standards and safety requirements, and proposals for demand-side incentives. To avoid a fragmented market, European standardisation bodies are developing a common charging system for electric cars, scooters and bicycles.

A German Intercity-Express (ICE) alongside a Eurostar at St Pancras International Station in London, in October. Further measures are being taken to turn the single European railway area into reality.

Rail

The EU also took further steps towards a single European railway area. This will result in better rail services for passengers and freight in the future. Rail freight in Europe was given a boost with new rules designed to foster the development of a high-quality rail infrastructure management at international level. These rules were published in October in the *Official Journal of the European Union*, making it mandatory to create a European rail network for competitive freight based on international freight corridors. This will help to reinforce cooperation between infrastructure managers and make rail freight services more competitive and attractive.

Further construction of the trans-European transport network was promoted by improving the information flow between Member States, the EU and investors. Nine new strategic corridors for rail freight were designated. In June, the Commission took legal action against 13 Member States for failing to fully implement the first railway package.

Sea

The Commission adopted new rules to enhance and improve the performance of technical inspections of ships, including a set of regulations ensuring transparency and public information on the safety records of shipping companies, flag states and ship risk profiles ([42]). The rules will introduce, from the beginning of 2011, a new online register that will 'name and shame' shipping companies that are performing poorly on vital safety inspections, as well as identifying those with strong safety records. Companies and states which show up as poorly performing will be subject to more intensive, coordinated inspections in EU ports, while customers will be able to choose their shipping companies in full knowledge of their safety record.

At the same time, the European Maritime Safety Agency continued the development of advanced maritime information tools, like SafeSeaNet — the EU maritime traffic surveillance system — or Thetis — the EU port state control information database. These new tools represent a decisive step forward in maritime safety policy, and are at the core of a pan-European system of monitoring, coordination and analysis that will allow for a more effective use of resources in all EU Member States.

The mandate of the European Maritime Safety Agency was modified in September so that it is able to face the challenges inherent in today's world. A social agenda for maritime transport was prepared for 2011; it comprises actions to strike a fair balance between adequate employment conditions for seafarers and the competitiveness of the industry, and EU enforcement of related international conventions.

In October, the Council adopted a regulation enhancing rights of ship passengers, with particular attention to passengers with disabilities or reduced mobility. The regulation provides for compensation and assistance when a journey is cancelled or delayed. It also ensures non-discrimination against and appropriate assistance for disabled passengers.

ENDNOTES

[1] Presidency conclusions of the European Council, 11 December 2009 (http://www.consilium.europa.eu/uedocs/cmsUpload/st00006.en09.pdf).

[2] Commission communication — Delivering an area of freedom, security and justice for Europe's citizens — Action plan implementing the Stockholm programme (COM(2010) 171).

[3] Resolution of the European Parliament of 23 November 2010.

[4] http://europa.eu/rapid/pressReleasesAction.do?reference=IP/10/1720&format=HTML&aged=0&language=EN&guiLanguage=en

[5] Court of Justice ruling of 1.7.2010 in Case C-211/10 PPU Povse.

[6] https://e-justice.europa.eu

[7] Court of Justice ruling of 19.1.2010 in Case C-555/07 Kücükdeveci.

[8] Court of Justice ruling of 12.10.2010 in Case C-499/08 Ingeniørforeningen i Danmark.

[9] Commission communication — The social and economic integration of the Roma in Europe (COM(2010) 133).

[10] Commission communication — Towards an EU strategy on the rights of the child (COM(2006) 367).

[11] Article 21(1) TFEU specifies that this right may be subject to certain limitations and conditions.

[12] Court of Justice ruling of 2.3.2010 in Case C-135/08 Rottmann.

[13] http://eur-lex.europa.eu/JOHtml.do?uri=OJ:L:2010:195:SOM:EN:HTML

[14] Council Regulation (EC) No 881/2002 imposing certain specific restrictive measures directed against certain persons and entities associated with Usama bin Laden, the Al-Qaida network and the Taliban (OJ L 139, 29.5.2002).

[15] Court of Justice ruling of 29.4.2010 in Case C-340/08 M and Others.

[16] Court of Justice ruling of 29.6.2010 in Case C-550/09 E and F.

[17] General Court ruling of 9.9.2010 in Case T-348/07 Al-Aqsa v Council.

[18] Brussels, 24 November 2010, 16913/10, PRESSE 321.

[19] http://ec.europa.eu/anti-trafficking

[20] Court of Justice ruling of 17.6.2010 in Case C-31/09 Bolbol.

[21] Regulation (EC) No 717/2007 on roaming on public mobile telephone networks within the Community (OJ L 171, 29.6.2007).

[22] Court of Justice ruling of 8.6.2010 in Case C-58/08 Vodafone and Others.

[23] Directive 97/7/EC on the protection of consumers in respect of distance contracts (OJ L 144, 4.6.1997).

[24] Court of Justice ruling of 15.4.2010 in Case C-511/08 Heinrich Heine.

[25] Directive 2001/95/EC on general product safety (OJ L 11, 15.1.2002).
Council Directive 87/357/EEC concerning products which, appearing to be other than they are, endanger the health or safety of consumers (OJ L 192, 11.7.1987).
Commission Decision 2010/11/EU on the safety requirements to be met by European standards for consumer-mounted childproof locking devices for windows and balcony doors (OJ L 4, 8.1.2010).
In May, the Commission asked the European Standardisation Committee to develop European safety standards for these products.

[26] Court of Justice ruling of 22.4.2010 in Case C-62/09 Association of the British Pharmaceutical Industry.

[27] Court of Justice ruling of 1.6.2010 in Joined Cases C-570/07 and C-571/07 Blanco Pérez and Chao Gómez.

[28] Court of Justice ruling of 15.6.2010 in Case C-211/08 Commission v Spain.

[29] Court of Justice ruling of 14.9.2010 in Case C-550/07 P Akzo Nobel Chemicals and Akcros Chemicals v Commission.

[30] Court of Justice ruling of 29.6.2010 in Case C-441/07 P Alrosa.

[31] General Court ruling of 9.9.2010 in Case T-155/06 Tomra Systems and Others v Commission.

[32] Court of Justice ruling of 14.10.2010 in Case C-280/08 P Deutsche Telekom v Commission.

[33] General Court ruling of 1.7.2010 in Case T-321/05 AstraZeneca v Commission.

[34] General Court rulings of 6.7.2010 in Case T-342/07 Ryanair v Commission and in Case T-411/07 Aer Lingus Group v Commission.

[35] Court of Justice rulings of 1.7.2010 in Case C-194/08 Gassmayr and in Case C-471/08 Parviainen.

[36] Economic and Financial Affairs Council conclusions, 17 November 2010 (http://www.consilium.europa.eu/uedocs/cms_data/docs/pressdata/en/lsa/117761.pdf).

[37] Court of Justice ruling of 13.4.2010 in Case C-73/08 Bressol and Others.

[38] Proposal for a decision establishing a European Union action for the European heritage label (COM(2010) 76).

[39] Education, Youth, Culture and Sport Council conclusions, 18 and 19 November 2010 (http://www.consilium.europa.eu/uedocs/cms_data/docs/pressdata/en/educ/117799.pdf).

[40] Convention for the Unification of Certain Rules for International Carriage by Air, concluded in Montreal on 28 May 1999.

[41] Court of Justice ruling of 6.5.2010 in Case C-63/09 Walz.

[42] http://europa.eu/rapid/pressReleasesAction.do?reference=IP/10/1115&format=HTML&aged=0&language=EN&guiLanguage=en
http://europa.eu/rapid/pressReleasesAction.do?reference=MEMO/10/401&format=HTML&aged=1&language=EN&guiLanguage=en

CHAPTER 3
ENERGY, CLIMATE
AND ENVIRONMENT

The European Union played a pioneering role during 2010 to ensure security of supply of energy for Europe, to tackle climate change at global level and to protect the environment for future generations. EU energy policy aims to create a competitive internal energy market offering quality service at low prices. The three priorities are developing renewable energy sources, reducing dependence on imported fuels, and energy efficiency — doing more with a lower consumption of energy.

The EU leads the world in tackling climate change. At home it has pioneered practical action to cap emissions and introduced the first major emissions trading system on the planet. In international negotiations, it has maintained its targets for 2020 and beyond to reduce greenhouse gas emissions. Furthermore, it has promoted links with other carbon trading systems with the ultimate aim of building an international carbon trading market. The emissions reduction targets that the EU has taken on will drive modernisation of the EU economy as well as help combat climate change.

Across the spectrum of problems related to waste, pollution, air and water quality, as well as in strategic issues like biodiversity, the EU has demonstrated its determination to make the European economy more environmentally friendly.

These efforts are integral to the Europe 2020 strategy, with its focus on smart, sustainable and inclusive growth. It is a strategic objective of the strategy to reinforce EU leadership in global moves to cut greenhouse gas emissions, through political pressure and innovation in low-carbon technologies. So too is the full deployment of EU research strengths in a shift towards a greener and more socially responsive economy. The benefits extend to citizens across the Member States, too — such as through the development of advanced combustion engines that reduce fuel consumption, or farming methods that provide high-quality food while preserving the countryside.

ENERGY

Europe needs a secure supply of energy at affordable prices in order to maintain standards of living. EU policy aims to create a competitive internal energy market that offers quality service at low prices. Specific goals include developing low-carbon energy sources and reducing dependence on imported fuels. Underpinning those goals is the objective of increasing economic activity while decreasing consumption of energy.

The EU is acting to complete the internal market for energy, to build and interconnect energy grids, and to ensure energy security, including across borders. It is doing for energy what has already been done for other services in the single market, from air travel to mobile phones: real choice for consumers in one European marketplace. The aim is a genuine energy community in Europe, where frontiers are irrelevant for pipelines or power cables, and where there is an infrastructure for solar and wind energy. Charging electric car batteries needs to be as natural as filling up the petrol tank.

Electricity power station. Ensuring Europe's energy supply.

In November the Commission presented 'Energy 2020 — A strategy for competitive, sustainable and secure energy'([1]), defining the EU's energy policy for the next 10 years. The strategy identified actions to save energy, achieve a market with competitive prices and security of supply. It envisages investment incentives for householders and local entities for energy-saving measures. It encourages the public sector to take energy efficiency into consideration when buying works, services or products. And it promotes certification schemes in the industrial sector to promote investment in technology which uses less energy.

The strategy sets a target date of 2015 for completing the internal energy market, and outlines a new approach to the way the EU plans to finance and implement energy infrastructure investment. It is estimated that over the next 10 years, overall energy infrastructure investments of €1 trillion will be needed in the EU. It also envisages a set of initiatives to strengthen research and technological development in energy, and to strengthen the EU's ability to negotiate with international partners. The first European Council of 2011 will be dedicated to Europe's future energy challenge.

Safety in energy provision also forced itself on to the agenda. In the wake of the Gulf of Mexico disaster, the European Union and individual Member States offered additional equipment to help contain the oil spill. Furthermore, the Commission published a communication on safety of offshore oil and gas activities [2] in order to minimise the risk of a similar disaster occurring. The aim is to ensure uniformly high safety standards and clear liabilities in offshore drilling operations across the EU, as well as environmental protection and emergency preparedness and response. This was the first time comprehensive EU legislation on oil and gas offshore installations had been envisaged. The new EU standards considered will include common criteria for granting drilling permits, controls of the installations, and safety control mechanisms. They not only seek the highest safety standards in European waters, but also aim at promoting them in adjacent regions and worldwide.

ENERGY INFRASTRUCTURE

Energy infrastructures are the vascular system of a modern economy. The ageing system in Europe is unfit to support the transition to a low-carbon resource-efficient energy production system. The lack of interconnection between national energy markets makes it difficult to realise a real single energy market that ensures fair competition and lower prices. For this reason, modernising the energy infrastructure system was high on the EU's agenda throughout 2010. In November, the Commission adopted energy infrastructure priorities for the next two decades [3]. It identified EU priority corridors for power grids and gas pipelines, to serve as a basis for future permit granting and financing decisions on EU projects. Infrastructure is recognised as an essential factor in achieving EU energy plans, in everything from the completion of the internal market to competitiveness and better service to consumers, from energy solidarity to meeting climate and renewable energy targets, and from energy efficiency to security of supply, both internally and externally. The Commission also incorporated ideas on how to harmonise investment rules in the EU and attract private financing.

Preparations were facilitated by a review in July of the implementation of trans-European energy networks during 2007–09. These were established to support completion of the internal energy market, to reduce isolation of remote regions, to secure and diversify energy supplies, and to contribute to sustainable development and environmental protection. More generally, the Commission looked into ways of improving regulatory coordination and cooperation across borders.

To improve transparency and enable adequate analysis of the EU's energy system, a new regulation adopted in June sets up the monitoring of investment projects in a wide range of production, transmission and storage infrastructure for oil (including biofuels), gas, electricity and carbon dioxide.

ENERGY EFFICIENCY

There was new impetus for energy efficiency, based on setting national targets consistent with the European headline target of a 20 % increase. Energy labelling was extended from household appliances to all energy-related products[4]. The first delegated regulations establishing requirements for the energy labelling of four household energy-related products were adopted[5].

Modernisation of the Romanian Parliament, one of the biggest buildings in the world, has included a new lighting system in which more than 31 000 lamps received energy-efficient light bulbs, leading to major savings in energy.

As part of the implementation of the 2009 ecodesign directive, the Commission adopted requirements for priority products that have an impact on energy consumption, such as industrial fans and domestic dishwashing machines. Work continued to create future requirements for more than 20 product groups. The EU also agreed new rules in May on the energy performance of buildings[6], strengthening and extending the current rules and reducing differences between Member States' control mechanisms on energy needs for devices such as space and hot-water heating, cooling, ventilation and lighting.

ELENA FACILITY

In order to enable committed cities and regions to unlock local and regional sustainable energy investments, the ELENA technical assistance facility, launched in 2009, in cooperation with the EIB, is likely to mobilise investments in excess of €1.3 billion, as a result of €17.5 million provided so far in technical assistance grants. In Barcelona, a contribution of €2 million is mobilising investment of €500 million; in Milan, €2 million should mobilise €90 million; in Purmerend in the Netherlands, an ELENA contribution of €1.7 million is leading to investment of €98 million. And in Paris, €1.3 million should mobilise €180 million.

Energy efficiency was successfully promoted at local level, too. In April the EU's GreenLight and GreenBuilding awards were presented to towns and buildings that achieve high energy savings. One of the 12 award winners in the 2010 edition of the GreenLight programme was Dagda Town Council in Latvia, which reduced its energy consumption in lighting by 85 % after joining the initiative in 2007. In the GreenBuilding category, two of the best refurbishment projects, an office building in Austria and a secondary school in Germany, have achieved energy savings of over 80 %. More than 700 participants all over Europe take part in these initiatives, saving over 500 GWh each year.

In May 2010, a further 500 cities pledged to reduce their carbon dioxide emissions by more than 20 % by 2020. By signing the Covenant of Mayors, they committed themselves to save energy, foster renewable energy and raise awareness among their citizens, through development and implementation of their sustainable energy action plans.

The Covenant of Mayors is a Commission initiative, supported both by the European Parliament and the Committee of the Regions. The city of Heidelberg for example has reduced its carbon dioxide emissions from public buildings by nearly 40 % through energy monitoring stations and the 'energy teams' in the city's schools. The city of Riga utilises the methane gas produced in the city's waste tip to produce electricity, and Antwerp uses a refurbished industrial warehouse as a showcase for sustainable building and a demonstration centre for citizens. So far, over 2 100 cities in 36 countries have joined the initiative, supported by over 100 regions, provinces and networks, representing over 125 million citizens.

RENEWABLE ENERGY SOURCES AND TECHNOLOGIES

The EU has set out over the past two years a comprehensive policy and legal framework for the development of renewable energy, as required by the renewable energy directive that entered into force in 2009. Member States drew up national renewable energy action plans in 2010 which provide a stable policy framework for investors for the next decade. These plans confirmed the potential for renewable energy use in the EU and the overall ability of the EU to reach or even slightly exceed the 20 % target by 2020.

Renewables are already having an impact in the EU's energy mix. They accounted for 62 % of the new electricity generation capacity installed in the EU in 2009 [7] — up from 57 % in 2008. For the second year running, wind energy accounted for the largest share of the new capacity: 10.2 GWh out of the 27.5 GWh built, representing 38 % of output. In absolute terms, renewables produced 19.9 % of Europe's electricity consumption in 2009.

In the field of renewable energy research, four European industrial initiatives were launched under the strategic energy technology plan (SET-Plan). These first initiatives cover wind energy, solar energy, electricity grids and carbon capture and storage. The public and private sector are engaged in accelerating the development of low-carbon technologies and have agreed to support technology roadmaps for 2010–20, including action plans to develop the technologies and improve their competitiveness.

In 2010, operations started under the European energy programme for recovery, launched in 2009 as a response to the economic and financial crisis in Europe. This stimulates diversification of energy supply, the operation of the internal energy market and the reduction of greenhouse gas emissions. It provides loans, guarantees and equity to projects in energy efficiency and renewable energy sources conducted by local governments, provinces, municipalities and private entities acting on behalf of public entities. As soon as the break-even point is achieved on each project, the loan is repaid into the fund.

2020 EMISSIONS COMPARED WITH 2005 (%).

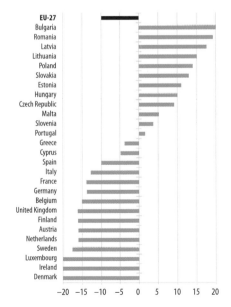

Source: European Commission.

Total finance of €3 980 million supports three sub-programmes: €2 365 million to gas and electricity infrastructure projects; €565 million to offshore wind electricity projects; and €1 050 million to carbon capture and storage projects. Beneficiaries had received €900 million by the end of the year. As project developers start to purchase building materials and construction works, the programme is already accelerating infrastructure investments, and attracting co-financers to make investment commitments. Unspent funds at the end of the year will be devoted to energy efficiency projects. In October, the Parliament and Council reached an agreement to reallocate €146 million of funds left uncommitted under the programme to an innovative financial instrument for energy efficiency and renewable energy initiatives.

ENERGY RECOVERY PROGRAMME

The EU funded 44 projects in the gas and electricity sectors with more than €2 billion during the year, and offshore wind projects of around €565 million.

The European Commission continued developing its support mechanisms for the commercial demonstration of carbon capture and storage (CCS) to verify the efficacy of this potentially vital climate change mitigation tool. CCS has the potential to contribute both to the EU's climate goals and to its security of energy supply. It is the only technology available for significantly cutting CO_2 emissions from fossil-fuelled power stations and large stationary industrial applications. In the EU the CO_2 emissions avoided through CCS in 2030 could account for some 15 % of the reductions required. In addition, CCS could significantly reduce climate change mitigation costs. A decision laying down criteria and measures for the financing of large-scale CCS projects, as well as innovative renewable energy technologies, under the emissions trading system was adopted in 2010 and followed up with a call for proposals [8]. At least eight major CCS demonstration projects could be financed by this scheme, with the first projects awarded funding in 2012. The CCS project network, a tool for supporting early large-scale demonstration of CCS technologies, was launched. This is the world's first network to foster knowledge sharing and raise public understanding of the role of CCS in cutting CO_2 emissions.

EMISSIONS ARE TRADED MORE

Volume in greenhouse gas emissions traded under the EU's Emission Trading System

Million tonnes of CO_2

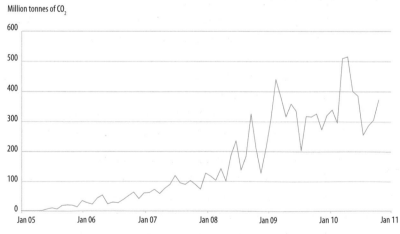

Source: European Commission.

NUCLEAR ENERGY

Nuclear energy is increasingly perceived as an important part of a balanced energy mix as it substantially contributes to low-carbon energy generation in the EU and to achieving EU energy policy objectives for 2020 and 2050. The EU cannot prescribe the choice of the national energy mix, but it does have the task of supporting at European level research and safety. Member States have a total of 143 nuclear power plants, and more are taking steps to launch, relaunch or further develop nuclear energy. Nuclear safety attracts public attention, and a solid legal framework and a deeply rooted nuclear safety culture are becoming even more important. Consequently, in November the Commission proposed (⁹) safety standards for final disposal of fuel and radioactive waste from nuclear power plants. Member States are asked to present national programmes, indicating when, where and how they will construct and manage final repositories aimed at guaranteeing the highest safety standards. The directive makes internationally agreed safety standards legally binding and enforceable in the European Union.

INTERNATIONAL RELATIONS AND SECURITY OF ENERGY SUPPLY

A new regulation on the security of gas supply (¹⁰) in the EU reduced the EU's vulnerability to future disruptions. Member States now have to comply with infrastructure and supply standards, and to establish preventive action plans and emergency plans. The proposal was prompted by the 2008 and 2009 gas crises, when supplies of Russian gas through Ukraine to the EU were disrupted by disputes between Moscow and Kiev. In September the European Parliament approved the new regulation on the security of gas supply, a major step forward towards a real European common energy policy that will also reduce vulnerability to future gas supply disruptions in crisis situations.

With both energy consumption and dependency on oil and gas imports growing and supplies becoming scarcer, the risk of supply failure is rising. Securing European energy supplies is therefore high on the EU's agenda. In addition to promoting energy efficiency to get the most out of supplies, the EU promotes a broad mix of energy sources, as well as diversity in suppliers, transport routes and transport mechanisms. Safeguard mechanisms increasingly secure energy supply for European citizens and industries. And reliable partnerships are built with supplier, transit and consumer countries, reducing the risks of Europe's energy dependency. Member States must keep emergency stocks of gas and oil and ensure investments in electricity networks, while a coordination mechanism now helps Member States react uniformly and immediately in an emergency.

Security of energy supplies was pursued through domestic legislation and by developing new cooperation and supply routes through international dialogue. The 10th anniversary of the EU–Russia Energy Dialogue (¹¹) provided an opportunity to enhance and update cooperation with the EU's most important energy supplier. The EU–Russia early warning mechanism agreed in November 2009 was successfully used for the first time during the June gas transit crisis with Belarus.

WHAT TYPE OF FUELS DO WE USE IN THE EU?
Share of fuels used to make energy in the 27 EU countries, 2008

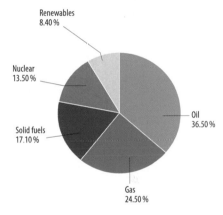

Source: European Commission.

WHERE DOES THE GAS COME FROM?
Sources of the natural gas used in the 27 EU countries, 2007

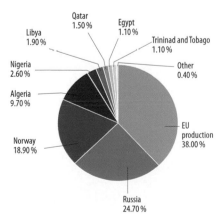

Source: European Commission.

The seventh ministerial-level meeting of the Energy Dialogue between the EU and the Organisation of the Petroleum Exporting Countries ([12]) underlined the role that the dialogue has been playing in facilitating constructive exchanges between the parties to help restore stability to the markets, in the interests of producers and consumers alike. In the framework of the Cooperation Agreement of the EU with the Gulf Cooperation Council, energy has a preponderant role in particular on natural gas trade between the two regions, energy efficiency, renewable energy sources and carbon capture and storage policies and technologies. The EU also pursued negotiations with the countries of the Maghreb on integration of energy markets — with a view to subsequent links with the EU. Efforts to diversify sources of supply also included signature of a memorandum of understanding on energy cooperation with Iraq, implementation of cooperation with existing suppliers and transit countries such as OPEC or countries in the central Asia/Black Sea area, and work in support of priority infrastructure projects such as the Southern Corridor. The EU supported further market integration with willing countries in the framework of the Energy Community Treaty, of which Moldova became a full member; Ukraine was in the process of ratifying its accession protocol; and Turkey continued negotiations on its accession.

The Commission paid particular attention to supporting low-carbon development in bilateral relations and through multilateral channels. With China, for example, relations intensified significantly, focusing on supporting China's low-carbon activities, as well as on promoting a level playing field for energy cooperation and transparent and stable market conditions in the Chinese energy sector.

Low-carbon technology is also one of the main topics addressed by the recently established EU–US Energy Council. Energy is an important component of EU–US dialogue, because it impacts foreign, economic and development policies. By working together on energy, mutual security and prosperity are increased, stable, reliable and transparent global energy markets are underpinned, and regulatory regimes and research programmes are coordinated to speed the deployment of tomorrow's clean and efficient energy technologies. The cooperation supports economic growth and job creation, and advances climate change goals.

AN EFFICIENT MARKET

The EU also acted to ensure that the energy market functioned efficiently. EU rules aim at increasing the capacity and transparency of gas and electricity markets. A properly functioning, well regulated, transparent and interconnected market with market price signals is crucial for ensuring competition and security of supply. An efficient and fully functional EU single market in energy will give consumers a choice between different companies supplying gas and electricity at reasonable prices, and it will make the market accessible for all suppliers, especially the smallest and those investing in renewable energies. It could also help the EU to recover from the economic crisis.

In July the Commission requested that Poland refrain from violating EU rules on the internal gas market. Infringements included obliging gas importers to store a certain percentage of gas in Poland, and the lack of access to the Yamal pipeline. The arrangements were adapted in line with EU law, and in November the Commission approved the new approach. In June the Commission sent 35 separate requests to 20 Member States to implement and apply in full various aspects of EU legislation to create a single market for gas and electricity. In May commitments made by E.On, in response to Commission pressure, helped open up the German energy market.

Making markets function efficiently means taking account of consumer interests, and in December the Council adopted conclusions on an 'Energy policy for consumers'([13]), dealing with aspects related to consumer rights and the protection of vulnerable customers, and taking into account contributions from the informal meeting of energy ministers held in September.

The year 2010 was one of preparation for the establishment of a European Agency for Cooperation of Energy Regulators — a strong agency capable of facing the multiple challenges of regulating the European energy market. It held its constituent meetings in the first half of 2010, and selected Ljubljana as its seat.

CLIMATE ACTION

The EU's commitments to climate action — already adopted well in advance of the UN Climate Change Conference in Copenhagen at the end of 2009 — were implemented throughout 2010, in the framework of its climate and energy package. The EU is championing the global efforts to implement ambitious, legally binding climate action — and is ready to move further.

In January the EU formally associated itself with the Copenhagen Accord that was negotiated at the end of the UN Climate Change Conference in December 2009. As agreed under the accord, Europe also formally notified its greenhouse gas emissions reduction targets for 2020 — a unilateral cut of 20 % below 1990 levels and an offer to scale this up to 30 % if other major economies commit to undertake their fair share of a global effort.

In line with its commitments, the EU made further progress towards meeting its Kyoto Protocol emission targets for 2012. The European Union is ahead of schedule in its promise to cut emissions. The Commission's assessment is that both the EU-15, the group of 'older' Member States, and the 10 'new' Member States which have reduction targets under the Kyoto Protocol will meet their commitments.

CLIMATE ACTION TARGETS

The EU's 20-20-20 targets for the year 2020, proposed in 2007 and agreed in 2008, signify a 20 % cut in greenhouse gas emissions from 1990 levels, a 20 % share for renewable energy and a 20 % reduction in energy use against projected levels through a major improvement in energy efficiency.

The cornerstone of EU climate policy, the emissions trading system (ETS), continued to evolve as preparations were made for the revised scheme that will take effect from 2013. New technical rules were decided, including the cap on emission allowances for 2013 [14] and rules for the auctioning of allowances [15], which will become the main method of allocation from 2013. In addition, the Commission submitted proposals for performance benchmarks for allocating free allowances to specific industry sectors [16]; and for a ban on the use of international credits from certain industrial gas projects post-2012 [17], which are a number of concerns. Meanwhile, emissions from the roughly 11 000 installations currently covered by the ETS have been falling: figures relating to 2009 [18] showed an 11.6 % drop from a year earlier [19]. And, in an important ruling, the General Court dismissed an action brought by a company challenging the validity of the emissions trading directive [20], which was adopted in order to promote reductions of greenhouse gas emissions, in particular CO_2, based on the Union's obligations under the United Nations Framework Convention on Climate Change and the Kyoto Protocol [21].

The EU also continued preparations for aviation's entry into the scheme [22]; from 1 January 2012 emissions from aircraft that fly in and out of airports in the EU will be included. The Commission also approved a tool [23] to estimate fuel consumption by small aircraft operators, allowing operators with few flights or low emissions to use simplified monitoring procedures. At international level, the EU was instrumental in securing recognition that actions can be taken now to reduce aviation's greenhouse gas impacts, and international agreement was reached that global greenhouse gas emissions from the sector should be reduced from 2020.

NER300: FUNDING INNOVATIVE LOW-CARBON TECHNOLOGIES

The ETS will benefit from a new EU financing instrument known as NER300 [24], the programme will provide substantial financial support for at least eight projects using carbon capture and storage technologies and at least 34 projects involving renewable energy technologies. The funding will come from the sale of 300 million EU ETS allowances (rights to emit 1 tonne of carbon dioxide) which at current prices could raise approximately €4.5 billion. NER300 aim is to drive low-carbon economic development in Europe, creating new 'green' jobs and contributing to the achievement of the EU's climate change goals. The European Investment Bank is collaborating with the Commission in implementation of the programme.

Moves were also made to impose limits on CO_2 emissions from vans. The European Parliament, Council and Commission reached an informal agreement on legislation in December which was rapidly endorsed by EU environment ministers. A discussion was launched on possible further moves to reduce EU emissions. The Commission presented an analysis [25] of the costs, benefits and options for moving beyond a 20 % reduction by 2020 once the conditions are met. The assessment found that the recession has considerably reduced the cost of meeting the 20 % target but that it also means the carbon price is likely to stay low for years to come, reducing the stimulus for low-carbon innovation. The extra 'cost' is an investment that will pay dividends — in terms of strengthening Europe's innovation and competitiveness, safeguarding jobs, reducing the energy import bill and boosting energy security, and cutting air pollution and its cost. The October Environment Council asked the Commission to elaborate further on the options.

The reflections on future emission reductions extend way beyond 2020. The EU's long-term target is to reduce its emissions by 80–95 % below 1990 levels by 2050. In this context a public consultation was held to help prepare a roadmap, to be issued in early 2011 as part of the Europe 2020 resource efficiency flagship initiative, for completing the transition to a low-carbon economy by 2050. A separate public consultation examined whether emissions and removals from the atmosphere of carbon dioxide and other greenhouse gases related to land use, land-use change and forestry should be covered by the EU's reduction target.

FROM COPENHAGEN TO CANCÚN

International negotiations aimed at establishing a global climate agreement under UN auspices continued during 2010. For the EU the priority In the early part of the year was to reinvigorate the negotiations after the disappointing outcome of the Copenhagen conference in December 2009. The Copenhagen Accord did, however, endorse the objective of keeping the increase in global temperatures below 2 °C above the pre-industrial level. The EU remains convinced that the only effective way to secure this objective is through a comprehensive legally binding global agreement, and during the year it helped build pressure accordingly. A Commission communication [26] in March proposed: swift EU implementation of the Copenhagen Accord, in particular the 'fast-start' financial assistance pledged to developing countries; taking a stepwise approach to reaching a global agreement; demonstrating EU leadership by taking tangible action to become the most climate friendly region of the world as part of the Europe 2020 strategy; and stepping up EU outreach to partners around the world to build confidence that a global deal under UN auspices remains possible.

The EU worked throughout the year to make the Cancún Climate Change Conference in November and December 2010 a further milestone on the road towards a legally binding international agreement. Negotiators met in Bonn in August, but with fewer results than had been hoped for. The final preparatory session for Cancún, in Tianjin, China, in early October, reached a broad consensus that Cancún should deliver a balanced package of decisions.

© David de la Paz / Belga

The EU worked throughout the year to make the UN Climate Change Conference in Cancún in November and December a further milestone on the road towards an international legal agreement.

The October Environment Council [27] and European Council [28] set out the EU's position for Cancún. Among other things, the Environment Council confirmed the EU's stepwise approach, set out the EU position on a global scheme for reducing emissions from tropical deforestation and on fast-start and long-term financing for developing countries. It also addressed EU expectations for strengthening the transparency of country actions on emissions and finance for improving carbon markets. The European Council underlined the importance of delivering a significant intermediate step, building on the Kyoto Protocol and paving the way towards a global and comprehensive legally binding framework. It also confirmed the EU's willingness to consider a second commitment period under the Kyoto Protocol provided Europe's conditions were met.

The December Economic and Financial Affairs Council ([29]) endorsed a report on the EU's progress in mobilising the €7.2 billion of fast-start funding it has pledged over 2010–12. This report was presented in Cancún, and the EU is committed to continuing to report transparently on implementation of its fast-start financing pledge on an annual basis.

PROTECTING THE FORESTS

The Paris–Oslo process on reducing emissions from deforestation and forest degradation in developing countries was formally launched at the end of May.

THE CANCÚN OUTCOME

The EU delegation went to Cancún to obtain a substantial package of action-oriented decisions and keep the international climate change negotiations on track. The conference held from 29 November to 10 December achieved these goals by producing the Cancún agreements. The EU welcomed the agreements as an important step towards a global framework for climate action. Europe succeeded in speaking with one voice and helped to deliver the successful outcome. The Commission acted in close contact with the Council and with the support of the European Parliament.

© Antonio Scorza / AFP / Belga

The EU supports action both in Europe and worldwide, in a bid to halt biodiversity loss and devastation like this burnt-out sector of the Jamanxim National Forest at an illegal settlement in northern Brazil.

The Cancún agreements build on the decisions taken in Copenhagen and set out processes for further progress. Key elements include:

▸ acknowledgement for the first time in a UN document that global warming must be kept below 2 °C compared to the pre-industrial temperature, and establishment of a process to define a date for global emissions to peak and a global emissions reduction goal for 2050;

▸ anchoring the emission pledges of developed and developing countries in the UN process, and helping clarify them; the text also recognises that overall mitigation efforts need to be scaled up in order to stay within the 2 °C ceiling;

▸ agreement to launch a process to strengthen the transparency of actions to reduce or limit emissions through better monitoring, reporting and verification so that overall progress can be tracked more effectively;

▸ confirmation of the goal that developed countries will mobilise US$100 billion in climate funding for developing countries annually by 2020, and establishment of a Green Climate Fund through which much of the funding will be channelled;

▸ agreement on the Cancún adaptation framework, to enhance action on adaptation to climate change;

▸ launch of a 'REDD+' mechanism enabling action to reduce emissions from deforestation and forest degradation in developing countries;

▸ establishment of a technology mechanism to enhance cooperation in technology development and transfer.

ENVIRONMENT

The 20th century provided phenomenal growth for Europe: a fourfold growth in population accompanied by a 40-fold growth in economic output. But it was highly resource-intensive: use of fossil fuels increased 16 times, fishing catches 35 times, water use 9 times and carbon emissions 17 times.

BIODIVERSITY

The EU Heads of State or Government adopted a new 2050 vision for biodiversity, along with a headline target that includes halting biodiversity loss by 2020 and maximising the restoration of biodiversity [30]. The EU has committed itself to protecting, valuing and restoring biodiversity and its ecosystem services, since they are essential to human well-being and economic prosperity. The aim is to integrate biodiversity concerns into all relevant policy areas — notably agriculture, fisheries, development and research, so that these sectors proactively contribute to the achievement of biodiversity objectives. The commitment has already produced action. New EU tools were unveiled in June to step up the fight against biodiversity loss, including a web portal [31] centralising information about European biodiversity, and a 'biodiversity baseline' that offers a comprehensive overview of the current state of biodiversity, to help policy-makers monitor progress in halting biodiversity loss. In October the Commission adopted a communication on integrating biodiversity and nature protection into port development, accompanied by environmental guidelines for ports. The communication in November on the future of the common agricultural policy [32] also looked towards 'greening' farm policy, and sustainability was one of the principal focuses of the preparations for the upcoming reform of the common fisheries policy [33].

Also, 2010 was the UN International Year of Biodiversity, and the EU welcomed the agreement it had promoted, at the 10th meeting of the Conference of the Parties to the Convention on Biological Diversity, in Nagoya in October, on a global strategy to combat biodiversity loss, the mobilisation of the necessary resources to implement it, and the creation of a protocol on access to and benefit sharing of genetic resources.

Attention to biodiversity also extends to reconciling its demands with other objectives of EU policy. For instance, poorly sited or designed wind farms can have a negative impact on vulnerable species and habitats. So the European Commission published guidelines [34] for wind energy development in protected natural areas.

GREEN WEEK 2010

In June, more than 3 000 participants from institutions, business and industry, non-governmental organisations, public authorities, the scientific community and academia attended the EU's Green Week 2010 in Brussels, Europe's largest annual conference on the environment. The year's theme, 'Biodiversity our lifeline', reflected the International Year of Biodiversity and concentrated on the variety of species and ecosystems that make up the web of life on the planet, and on the indispensable services provided by nature, including climate regulation. It showcased that investment in nature is a part of the solution, contributing to job provision and business opportunities.

COMBATING BIODIVERSITY LOSS

The EU has long been the world's leading financial donor in the battle against biodiversity loss. Since 2002 it has contributed almost €9 billion. It has the largest number of protected areas in the world — 26 000 of them, covering 18 % of its land area.

ENVIRONMENTAL SUSTAINABILITY

Sustainability featured high on the EU agenda all year as a central element in
Europe 2020. It is a consideration that permeates nearly all aspects of life, and EU
actions have consequently ranged widely.

One priority has been to protect the environment from damage caused by
waste and hazardous materials or emissions. Work progressed on recasts of
the waste electric and electronic equipment directive [35] and the directive to
restrict hazardous substances [36] — such as lead, mercury or cadmium — in
such equipment. The scope of the rules was also widened, to eliminate as far
as possible the use of hazardous substances, and to counter the fast-growing
volume of this type of waste, which has adverse environmental and health
consequences if not properly treated and disposed of.

Clearer rules and cleaner air are among the aims of the industrial emissions
directive, approved in November [37]. Stricter limits will apply for air pollution,
although with some flexibility on deadlines for power plants or special cases.
The directive updates and merges seven pieces of existing legislation, including
directives on large combustion plants and integrated pollution prevention and
control, and covers around 52 000 industrial and agricultural installations with a
high pollution potential, from refineries to pig farms.

Other actions have focused on preserving the natural environment. The illegal
timber regulation [38] controls imports, with the aim of preventing the sale
of illegal timber, or products made with such timber, on the EU market.
Illegal logging causes serious environmental damage and undermines the
efforts of those who are trying to manage forests responsibly. At the same time
the legislation helps in combating climate change.

The agreement on the biofuel and bioliquids sustainability scheme, as part of the
2009 renewable energy directive, ensured that financial support and counting
towards national renewable targets are only possible for biofuels meeting
sustainability criteria. This scheme is the first legally binding set of biofuel
sustainability criteria in the world, and is likely to be a pathfinder. To make it
fully effective, certification schemes operated by industry, governments and
NGOs are needed, and the Commission outlined a system [39] for recognising
sustainable biofuels that help deliver substantial reductions in greenhouse gas
emissions and do not come from forests, wetlands or nature protection areas.
The Commission also made recommendations on criteria for national schemes
on sustainability of solid biomass and biogas used in electricity, heating and
cooling, so as to promote an effective internal market for biomass.

© Gary Lee / Belga

*EU research funding supported
the HyFLEET:CUTE project.*

The EU also updated the rules on seeds and propagating material, in relation to the preservation of plant genetic resources and initiated evaluations of the Community regimes on plant variety rights and on plant health. And in July €250 million was allocated to 210 new projects under the LIFE+ programme [40], the European fund for the environment; the projects advance nature conservation, environmental policy, and information and communication.

The EU is constantly seeking the best balance between preserving the natural environment and ensuring growth and prosperity. For instance, the Commission proposed new ways of dealing with the continuing diverse views in Europe on controlling the cultivation of genetically modified organisms [41].

Protection for inhabitants of the natural environment has also been the focus of EU attention. New rules [42] require travellers who purchase seal products outside Europe to present a special declaration to the customs authorities on their return home, attesting that they come only from Inuit hunting. An animal testing directive [43] to reduce tests and provide better protection of animals used for research was adopted, updating the 1986 rules: it allows medical experiments with animals only if there are no alternatives; and all institutions conducting research with animals need to fulfil strict criteria and allow regular outside controls.

© EPA / Belga

The European Green Capital 2011 award was launched in Hamburg at one of the city's energy-efficient buildings.

SUSTAINABLE USE OF NATURAL RESOURCES AND SEAS

Sustainability is also at the heart of EU thinking as it prepares to change its fisheries policy. The recognition that a significant number of stocks are overfished is driving reform that will make the policy simpler and greener. It will push the fishing industry to take more responsibility and become more involved in decision-making and implementation, eliminating overcapacity and discards, and putting the fish stocks and ecosystem first. To make this a global reality, the EU now includes sustainable fisheries commitments in all EU free trade agreements.

High on the risk-list for exhaustion and depredation are natural resources and seas. A new Commission strategy[44] announced in May aims to improve the management of biowaste in the EU and tap into its significant environmental and economic benefits. And in September[45] the Commission set out criteria for a 'good environmental status' for Europe's seas, to help Member States develop coordinated marine strategies within each regional sea. Good environmental status means that the overall environment in marine waters provides ecologically diverse and dynamic oceans and seas which are healthy and productive. The definition of the criteria is a requirement under the marine strategy framework directive, which aims to achieve good environmental status in all EU marine waters by 2020. The definition focuses on biological diversity, fish population, eutrophication, contaminants, litter and noise.

The EU's integrated maritime policy[46] has also promoted Member States' use of the sea and coasts that respects the marine environment, and a cross-sectoral strategy is being constructed for sustainable growth of maritime sectors and coastal regions. The June European Council gave additional impetus to the development of strategies at the level of sea basins, and in October the Commission set out options for a common approach to maritime spatial planning across the EU, as well as an initiative to develop marine knowledge as an adjunct to the Europe 2020 strategy[47] in September. In November, the EU launched its first *Atlas of the seas*[48].

Policy has also been defined in the EU maritime transport strategy until 2018[49], to boost efforts to improve the environmental record of maritime transport through prevention of accidents, reduction of atmospheric emissions, controls on ballast water treatment, and ship recycling. The long-term objective is 'zero-waste, zero emissions' for maritime transport.

Fisheries are among the richest natural resources of the seas, and in January a new system[50] to better control fisheries and fight against illegal fishing entered into force. This provides the EU and its Member States with new tools to combat unscrupulous operators and to protect the livelihoods of honest fishermen who would otherwise be exposed to unfair competition. Because offenders are no longer allowed to avoid detection and punishment, a culture of compliance is being promoted throughout the fisheries sector. In June, a regulation on the conservation and sustainable exploitation of fisheries resources in the Mediterranean entered into force.

The October Fisheries Council reached a political agreement on fishing opportunities for 2011 in the Baltic Sea, and the November Fisheries Council obtained a political agreement on a regulation fixing for 2011 and 2012 the fishing opportunities for EU vessels for certain deep-sea stocks, and prepared to set EU/Norway annual total allowable catches for 2011. The December Fisheries Council reached agreement for fishing opportunities for 2011 in the Atlantic, North Sea and Black Sea. On the international stage, the EU worked to obtain a ban on trade in bluefin tuna, presenting a firm position at the meeting of the International Commission for the Conservation of Atlantic Tunas in November.

In addition to the pressure it exerted at international level to increase protection for Atlantic bluefin tuna, the Commission, the Community Fisheries Control Agency and the Member States implemented a new control and inspection programme and a comprehensive plan to prevent overfishing. Vessel-by-vessel and day-by-day monitoring of quota consumption has been conducted, the permitted fishing season was closed early, and EU fishing capacity was further reduced.

The recognition that land is a finite natural resource also prompted EU action on sustainability in everything from agriculture to transport and energy. Funding from the CAP health check and other monies within the CAP have helped bolster Member States' rural development programmes for addressing the challenges facing European farmers, such as taking account of biodiversity.

The blueprint for a forward-looking common agricultural policy [51], released in November, also makes sustainability a central priority — alongside viable food production and balanced territorial development. It aims to make European agriculture not only economically competitive, but also environmentally competitive. A public debate and a major conference on the future of the CAP during the year identified sustainable management of natural resources and climate action as one of the three principal objectives. Modified criteria for direct payments should include environmental considerations, reflecting the public goods provided by farmers, it concluded.

Sustainable transport has been advanced by projects ranging from networks to advanced research. For example, there is an untapped potential for increasing low-carbon mobility which can be unlocked if €5.5 billion of European funds earmarked for railways for the years 2007–13 are fully used. Moreover, the adoption at the end of the year of the regulation [52] related to a European rail network for competitive freight made it possible to promote improved use of the existing rail transport infrastructure, thus improving the efficiency and attraction of rail freight transport.

© Daniel Roland / AP / Reporters

Freight trains stand at a depot in Mannheim, Germany.

Keeping traffic moving and keeping pollution down are among the goals of the Eurovignette, the road charging system that links road transport with its impact on the environment.

The Eurovignette directive was revived[53] by adapting vehicle tax rates and road user charges to inflation, and providing additional links between road transport and its impact on the environment: Member State governments reached a political agreement on 15 October to allow the levying of tolls that factor in the cost of air and noise pollution and take account of road congestion. The Council also adopted a directive[54] laying down the framework for the deployment of intelligent transport systems, which increase efficiency and reduce environmental impact.

The seventh framework programme for research

As a whole, the seventh framework programme for research (FP7) supported over 120 projects in 2010 in the field of environment, energy and biotechnologies, with up to €450 million. The range is clearly illustrated by this selection of projects and initiatives that started in 2010:

Marina Platform — Marine Renewable Integrated Application Platform (EU contribution €8.7 million)

Silicon Light — Improved material quality and light trapping in thin film silicon solar cells (EU contribution €5.8 million)

Eurobioref — European multilevel integrated biorefinery design for sustainable biomass processing (EU contribution €23.1 million)

ICAP — Innovative CO_2 capture (EU contribution €4.3 million)

GHG Europe — Greenhouse gas management in European land use systems (estimated EC contribution €6 648 704)

STEP — Status and trends of European pollinators (estimated EU contribution €3 499 995).

ENDNOTES

(¹) Commission communication — Energy 2020 — A strategy for competitive, sustainable and secure energy (COM(2010) 639).

(²) Commission communication — Facing the challenge of the safety of offshore oil and gas activities (COM(2010) 560).

(³) Commission communication — Energy infrastructure priorities for 2020 and beyond — A blueprint for an integrated European energy network (COM(2010) 677).

(⁴) Directive 2010/30/EU on the indication by labelling and standard product information of the consumption of energy and other resources by energy-related products (OJ L 153, 18.6.2010).

(⁵) Delegated Regulations (EU) Nos 1059/2010, 1060/2010, 1061/2010 and 1062/2010 with regard to energy labelling of household dishwashers, household refrigerating appliances, household washing machines and televisions (OJ L 314, 30.11.2010).

(⁶) Directive 2010/31/EU on the energy performance of buildings (OJ L 153, 18.6.2010).

(⁷) *Renewable energy snapshots 2010* report published by the European Commission's Joint Research Centre on 5 July 2010 (http://re.jrc.ec.europa.eu/refsys/).

(⁸) The so-called New Entrants Reserve, or NER300, consists of 300 million EU emissions allowances.

(⁹) Proposal for a directive on the management of spent fuel and radioactive waste (COM(2010) 618).

(¹⁰) Regulation (EU) No 994/2010 concerning measures to safeguard security of gas supply (OJ L 295, 12.11.2010).

(¹¹) http://ec.europa.eu/energy/international/events/2010_11_22_eu_russia_anniversary_en.htm

(¹²) http://ec.europa.eu/energy/international/organisations/opec_en.htm

(¹³) An energy policy for consumers: Council conclusions, 29 October 2010 (http://register.consilium.europa.eu/pdf/en/10/st15/st15697.en10.pdf).

(¹⁴) Commission Decision 2010/634/EU adjusting the Union-wide quantity of allowances to be issued under the Union scheme for 2013 (OJ L 279, 23.10.2010).

(¹⁵) Commission Regulation (EU) No 1031/2010 on the timing, administration and other aspects of auctioning of greenhouse gas emission allowances (OJ L 302 18.11.2010).

(¹⁶) http://ec.europa.eu/clima/policies/ets/benchmarking_en.htm

(¹⁷) http://ec.europa.eu/commission_2010-2014/hedegaard/docs/proposal_restrictions_final.pdf

(¹⁸) http://europa.eu/rapid/pressReleasesAction.do?reference=IP/10/576&language=EN

(¹⁹) Commission report — Progress towards achieving the Kyoto objectives (COM(2010) 569).

(²⁰) Directive 2003/87/EC establishing a scheme for greenhouse gas emission allowance trading within the Community (OJ L 275, 25.10.2003).

(²¹) General Court ruling of 2.3.2010 in Case T-16/04 *Arcelor* v *Parliament and Council*.

(²²) Commission Decision 2009/339/EC as regards the inclusion of monitoring and reporting guidelines for emissions and tonne-kilometre data from aviation activities (OJ L 103, 23.4.2009).

(²³) http://www.eurocontrol.int/environment/public/standard_page/small_emitters.html

(²⁴) http://ec.europa.eu/clima/funding/ner300/index_en.htm

(²⁵) Commission communication — Analysis of options to move beyond 20 % greenhouse gas emission reductions and assessing the risk of carbon leakage (COM(2010) 265).

(²⁶) Commission communication — International climate policy post-Copenhagen: Acting now to reinvigorate global action on climate change (COM(2010) 86).

(²⁷) Environment Council conclusions, 14 October 2010 (http://www.consilium.europa.eu/uedocs/cms_data/docs/pressdata/en/envir/117096.pdf).

(²⁸) Presidency conclusions of the European Council, 28/29 October 2010 (http://www.consilium.europa.eu/uedocs/cms_data/docs/pressdata/en/ec/117496.pdf).

(²⁹) Economic and Financial Affairs Council conclusions, 17 November 2010 (http://www.consilium.europa.eu/uedocs/cms_data/docs/pressdata/en/ecofin/117790.pdf).

(³⁰) Presidency conclusions of the European Council, 25/26 March 2010 (http://www.consilium.europa.eu/uedocs/cms_data/docs/pressdata/en/ec/113591.pdf).

(³¹) http://biodiversity.europa.eu/

(³²) Commission communication — The CAP towards 2020: Meeting the food, natural resources and territorial challenges of the future (COM(2010) 672).

(³³) http://ec.europa.eu/fisheries/reform/index_en.htm: 'We have also started a broader assessment of the impact of the reform, which will be carried out according to the Commission's methodology for impact assessments. We will develop different scenarios for the future policy to evaluate the outcomes of different choices. We will focus in particular on the environmental, the economic and the social aspects in this impact assessment. This analysis will be used in preparation of the legal proposals for the reformed policy. According to our planning, the impact assessment should be finalised in autumn 2010.' (http://ec.europa.eu/fisheries/reform/sec(2010)0428_en.pdf)

(³⁴) http://ec.europa.eu/environment/nature/natura2000/management/docs/Wind_farms.pdf

(³⁵) Directive 2002/96/EC on waste electrical and electronic equipment (WEE) (OJ L 37, 13.2.2003).

(³⁶) Directive 2002/95/EC on the restriction of the use of certain hazardous substances in electrical and electronic equipment (OJ L 37, 13.2.2003).

(³⁷) Council approval, 8 November 2010 (http://www.consilium.europa.eu/uedocs/cms_data/docs/pressdata/en/envir/117566.pdf).

(³⁸) Regulation (EU) No 995/2010 laying down the obligations of operators who place timber and timber products on the market (OJ L 295, 12.11.2010).

(³⁹) Commission documents — system for certifying sustainable biofuels (http://ec.europa.eu/energy/renewables/biofuels/sustainability_criteria_en.htm).

(⁴⁰) http://europa.eu/rapid/pressReleasesAction.do?reference=IP/10/1002&format=HTML&aged=0&language=EN&guiLanguage=en

(⁴¹) Commission communication on the freedom for Member States to decide on the cultivation of genetically modified crops (COM(2010) 380).

(⁴²) Regulation (EC) No 1007/2009 on trade in seal products (OJ L 286, 31.10.2009).

(⁴³) Directive 2010/63/EU on the protection of animals used for scientific purposes (OJ L 276, 20.10.2010).

(⁴⁴) Commission communication on future steps in biowaste management in the European Union (COM(2010) 235).

(⁴⁵) Commission Decision 2010/477/EU on criteria and methodological standards on good environmental status of marine waters (OJ L 232, 2.9.2010).

(⁴⁶) Proposal for a regulation establishing a programme to support the further development of an integrated maritime policy (COM(2010) 494).

(⁴⁷) Ibid.

(⁴⁸) http://ec.europa.eu/maritimeaffairs/atlas/index_en.htm

(⁴⁹) Commission communication — Strategic goals and recommendations for the EU's maritime transport policy until 2018 (COM(2009) 8).

(⁵⁰) Commission Regulation (EC) No 1010/2009 laying down detailed rules for the implementation of Council Regulation (EC) No 1005/2008 establishing a Community system to prevent, deter and eliminate illegal, unreported and unregulated fishing (OJ L 280, 27.10.2009).

(⁵¹) Commission communication — The CAP towards 2020: Meeting the food, natural resources and territorial challenges of the future (COM(2010) 672).

(⁵²) Regulation (EU) No 913/2010 concerning a European rail network for competitive freight (OJ L 276, 20.10.2010).

(⁵³) Transport, Telecommunications and Energy Council — Political agreement, 15 October 2010 (http://register.consilium.europa.eu/pdf/en/10/st15/st15147.en10.pdf).

(⁵⁴) Directive 2010/40/EU on the framework for the deployment of intelligent transport systems in the field of road transport and for interfaces with other modes of transport (OJ L 207, 6.8.2010).

**CHAPTER 4
THE EU IN THE WORLD**

The Lisbon Treaty confers a new coherence on the EU's external relations. A new High Representative and Vice-President of the Commission was given responsibility for the foreign policy of the Union. In this role, Catherine Ashton chairs the Foreign Affairs Council and heads the new diplomatic service. This gives the Union the capacity to speak with one voice as well as the practical means to project its values better at global level: respect for human rights and democracy, cooperation to address common challenges and a commitment to multilateralism. Added to its strengths — as the world's biggest trader and biggest donor of aid, with a dense web of political and cultural connections and with a major international currency — the EU has improved its potential to become a key player on the world stage commensurate with its economic weight. Its new capacity for integrated engagement was demonstrated throughout the year, with its constructive responses to need in situations as diverse as Haiti, the occupied Palestinian territory or Darfur.

The creation of the European External Action Service, with the Union's delegations throughout the world, provides the backbone for new momentum to the Union's external relations. The European Council in September instituted the new approach, in which EU and national instruments and policies are mobilised in support of the Union's strategic interests. Also, a new form of leadership in international summits has been established with the President of the European Commission and the President of the European Council working in tandem.

The EU supports multilateral approaches, maintains close links with its strategic partners and strives for deeper bilateral relations and regional dialogues around the world. The EU projected its Europe 2020 recovery and growth strategy into the global market place, including through the G20. It addressed the challenges of energy geopolitics. It pursued the international development agenda and demonstrated in concrete actions its solidarity with the most vulnerable in the world.

PROMOTING MULTILATERAL GOVERNANCE

In pursuing its goals in a worldwide context, the EU supports multilateral institutions to protect the global common good and develop peace and prosperity worldwide.

In line with its engagement in support of an effective multilateral system, the EU has worked through the United Nations to promote peace, development and human rights, as well as to tackle new global challenges. The EU welcomed the agreement in June on modifications to the UN's structure and composition, including the creation of a single entity responsible for gender issues, and the review of the work of the Peacebuilding Commission. In other international organisations such as the International Monetary Fund, the World Bank, the World Trade Organisation, the Organisation for Economic Cooperation and Development, the Food and Agriculture Organisation and the United Nations Environment Programme, the EU has worked to promote multilateral approaches.

Accession negotiations with the European Convention on Human Rights and Fundamental Freedoms were started by the Commission in July (see Chapter 2), and an EU Delegation to the Council of Europe was set up in Strasbourg in October — an indication of deepening relations. In December, the EU played an active role in the organisation and preparation of the first summit of the Organisation for Security and Cooperation in Europe in 11 years, in Astana, under Kazakh chairmanship.

THE EU AT THE HEART OF THE G20

The EU is a prominent force in the G20 leaders' process, which was launched on a European initiative, when President Barroso and President Sarkozy visited the USA in 2008. It is today the primary forum for international economic coordination. It grew out of the G8, comprising Canada, France, Germany, Italy, Japan, Russia, the United Kingdom and the United States and at which the EU is also represented. The G20 brings together 19 countries plus the EU (the G8, plus Argentina, Australia, Brazil, China, India, Indonesia, Mexico, Saudi Arabia, South Africa, South Korea and Turkey).

The EU played an active role in major international forums, including the UN Human Rights Council and the UN General Assembly in September. The European Union was well represented in high-level meetings with world leaders, and with key countries and regional groupings. This reflected its commitment to achieving the millennium development goals as well as to using multilateralism to tackle the global challenges of development, peace and security, humanitarian crises and climate action.

In support of the UN, the EU implemented new UN Security Council sanctions in Somalia, Eritrea and Iran. The Commission also continued to represent the EU in the Kimberley Process, the UN-backed 75-country intergovernmental body for the prevention of trade in conflict diamonds. Supporting and indeed going beyond the UN resolution aimed at restraining Iran's nuclear ambitions, the EU imposed further sanctions in July, covering trade, financial services, energy, transport, visas and asset freezes wherever a connection with Iran's nuclear and ballistic programme exists ([1]). At the same time — crucially — the EU continued to lead efforts to find a negotiated agreement. The EU's High Representative acted as negotiator on behalf of the so-called E3+3 group of China, France, Germany, Russia, the United Kingdom and the United States.

A more effective, coherent and visible EU foreign policy

With the implementation of the Lisbon Treaty, the new High Representative of the Union for Foreign Affairs and Security Policy brings together what were previously three distinct jobs: the High Representative at the Council, the External Relations Commissioner at the Commission and — as did the rotating Presidency of the Council — chairing the meetings of EU foreign, development and defence ministers. As a Vice-President of the Commission, the High Representative helps to ensure consistency across the spectrum of EU external relations — and especially between political objectives and the EU's distinct spending and assistance programmes.

The new European External Action Service was forged during the year (²), and came into existence formally on 1 December. It unites the foreign policy capacities of the Commission with those of the Council and is supplemented with diplomats from the Member States, significantly reinforcing the EU's ability to play its international role. It is developing a highly skilled and fully integrated civil service at headquarters, and provides, for the first time, diplomatic representation of the EU itself in scores of countries around the world. The incorporation of Member State diplomats, with their experience of their own foreign services, brings valuable new synergies. The first senior appointments to the service and to key diplomatic posts — including from Member States — were made during the autumn.

STRENGTHENING STRATEGIC ALLIANCES

As the strategic partnerships of the 21st century emerge and the new world politics take shape, Europe is seizing the chance to contribute to shaping the globalised world. The relationships the EU builds with strategic partners are crucial in this respect. To be effective on the international stage, the EU needs strong alliances. To help it achieve its goals it maintains close relations with a number of leading countries that it considers strategic. There were major developments in many of these relations in 2010.

The **United States** continues to be the EU's closest and most important partner. The conclusions of the EU–US Summit in Lisbon in November (³) — the first since the entry into force of the Treaty of Lisbon — reaffirmed the close partnership. The EU and the USA not only share the same values, interests and objectives; together, they produce almost half of the world's GDP. The transatlantic economic partnership worth more than €3 000 billion is a driver of global economic prosperity and represents the largest, most integrated and far-sighted economic relationship in the world. The EU and the USA together provide approximately 80 % of official development assistance worldwide. During the year they cooperated effectively on foreign policy issues, including the Middle East peace process, Afghanistan and Pakistan, non-proliferation and regional conflicts. Regular dialogue on foreign policy takes place between EU High Representative Catherine Ashton and US Secretary of State Hillary Clinton.

AN EFFECTIVE EU–US PARTNERSHIP

The November summit focused on three areas of cooperation of vital interest to the combined 800 million citizens the two sides represent: growth and jobs; climate change and international development; and strengthening the security of citizens. The summit rejected protectionism and endorsed the concept of robust and transparent greenhouse gas emissions reduction commitments by major economies. It pledged to strengthen cooperation on the millennium development goals, and agreed on a more comprehensive and strategic approach to major international security issues. A joint working group on cybersecurity and cybercrime was established.

Regular dialogue on foreign policy takes place between EU High Representative Catherine Ashton and US Secretary of State Hillary Clinton.

© European Union

In addition, a further open skies aviation agreement (^{4}) was reached during the year, worth up to €12 billion in economic benefits and creating 80 000 new jobs, and deepening cooperation in aviation security, safety, competition and ease of travel. The agreement includes a novel article on the importance of high labour standards in the airline industry, and underscores the importance of transatlantic cooperation on aviation environmental matters.

Russian President Dmitri Medvedev, European Council President Herman Van Rompuy and European Commission President José Manuel Barroso at the EU–Russia Summit in Brussels.

With **Russia**, the dialogue was maintained through numerous channels. The EU–Russia Summit in Rostov-on-Don in June launched the partnership for modernisation (^{5}), aimed at promoting reform, boosting economic progress and raising competitiveness. This builds on results achieved so far in the context of the four common spaces (economic space, space of freedom, security and justice, space of external security, space of research and education, including cultural aspects), and brings a new urgency and result-oriented focus. Negotiations for a successor to the current partnership and cooperation agreement continued throughout the year. Human rights consultations between the EU and Russia were held twice in Brussels, in April and November. European Parliament President Jerzy Buzek visited Moscow in June, while direct contact between the Members of the European Parliament and their Russian counterparts continued via the meetings of the EU–Russia Parliamentary Cooperation Committee.

The entry into force of the Lisbon Treaty also opened a new chapter in the relations between the EU and **China**, enabling the EU to demonstrate a more coherent approach. The joint summit in October was approached by both sides in a spirit of reciprocity and mutual benefit. There was a shared interest to work together in strengthening bilateral relations through political dialogue, trade and investment. Mutual interest also prevailed in addressing global challenges, notably the financial and economic crisis and climate change and energy, in the run-up to the G20 Summit in Seoul in November and the Climate Change Summit in Cancún in December. An EU–China clean energy centre was opened in Beijing.

The range and intensity of EU relations with its key partners can also be gauged from a sample of the contacts during the year. A summit with **Canada** in May [6] rejected protectionism, and took stock of progress in negotiating an ambitious comprehensive economic and trade agreement that will give a new impetus to trade, investment, innovation and job creation. The EU–**India** Summit in Brussels in December emphasised the fight against terrorism (where an agreement between Europol and India is being negotiated, including a set of concrete measures), crisis management, maritime security, non-proliferation, peacebuilding and peacekeeping, as well as economic governance and regional issues within the south Asian region. Both sides also committed to increased cooperation in trade, with substantial progress made towards the signature of a free trade agreement, and in energy and climate change. The summit recognised the importance of a migration dialogue within the broader context of EU–India cooperation.

A summit with **Japan** in April [7] reaffirmed a shared commitment to combating climate change and to preserving biodiversity, and reached common understandings on regional issues including North Korea. In May, the EU and **South Korea** signed a new framework agreement for bilateral relations, an expression of common values and a basis for strengthened cooperation and dialogue across human rights, non-proliferation of weapons of mass destruction, counterterrorism, climate change and security of energy supply [8]. The bi-regional strategic partnership with **Latin America** and **the Caribbean** was strengthened at a summit in Madrid in May [9], deepening political dialogue and regional integration, promoting social cohesion and intensifying bilateral relations between individual countries from both regions (see page 95). It notably included the conclusion of the first region-to-region association agreement of the EU (with Central America), a trade agreement with Colombia and Peru, and the relaunching of the negotiations in view of an association agreement with Mercosur. The Latin American Investment Facility and the EU–LAC Foundation were also launched.

An EU–**Brazil** Summit took place in Brasilia in July, confirming the solidity of the bilateral relationship [10]. It explored climate change and the international economic and financial crisis, as well as the G20 process. Civil aviation agreements were signed, and a triangular cooperation initiative with Mozambique was launched in the field of bioenergy. An EU–**Mexico** Summit in May approved a new step in the strategic partnership [11], enhancing collaboration at bilateral and multilateral levels, including a focus on sectoral dialogues on security and law enforcement.

President of the European Council Herman Van Rompuy, President of Brazil Luiz Inacio Lula da Silva and President of the European Commission José Manuel Barroso at the EU–Brazil Summit in Brasilia.

The EU's international engagement led it to conclude agreements in areas of importance to citizens at home and around the world, notably in transport and in science and research. It reached aviation agreements, leading to more flights for passengers, higher safety standards and increased business opportunities. In addition to the bilateral open skies agreement with the USA and the safety agreement with Brazil (see page 88 and preceding paragraph), the EU and **Vietnam** signed an agreement in October which will remove nationality restrictions in bilateral air services [12]. Air safety and protection of the environment around the world were given a boost by cooperation at UN level through the International Civil Aviation Organisation.

A transport and logistics partnership was implemented in the Northern Dimension area, and a regulatory framework developed for the trans-Mediterranean transport network. The Commission helped to improve international rail standards and promote alignment with EU norms through its increased engagement with international rail organisations extending into Russia, north Africa and Asia. Progress towards high-quality shipping worldwide was assisted by EU involvement in international maritime negotiations, and pilot schemes for the EU's short sea shipping strategy are strengthening links between the EU and its close trading partners, improving maritime links and integration into door-to-door logistics chains. A conference on international shipping policies in Copenhagen in June brought together participants from the EU, Asia and North America.

Research cooperation extended across environmental research (such as the Soiltrec project with China and other countries to counter threats to soils from climate change and other pressures), health research (in the International Cancer Genome Consortium), engagement in the geopolitical forecasting exercise 'Global Europe in 2030–50', assessing the security of energy supply and the EU–China Science and Technology Week in Shanghai. In the area of food safety, the Commission has also coordinated Member States' input at the Office International des Epizooties, within the committees of the World Trade Organisation and — in relation to animal welfare — with the Council of Europe.

The EU was well represented at the 2010 Shanghai World Expo. It shared its pavilion with Belgium, the country that held the six-month rotating Presidency of the Council in the second half of the year.

PROMOTING PEACE, SECURITY AND HUMAN RIGHTS

Because its own origins and evolution are based on the establishment of peace and security, the EU remains committed to promoting these conditions beyond its borders too. Economic, political and social development around the world — and human rights too — depend on peace and security.

The EU has continued its engagement in conflict resolution and state-building processes in Afghanistan and Pakistan, not only for the benefit of local populations, but for Europeans too. It has worked to stabilise Afghanistan, with European soldiers, police, judges and other civilian personnel on the ground. They all contribute to building the institutions that improve the prospects of the state to function independently, and to establishing sustainable livelihoods that will allow communities to thrive beyond conflict and the drug trade. In Pakistan, which faces multiple challenges, including political, economic and institutional ones, the EU has deepened its engagement, as confirmed by the EU–Pakistan Summit in June. And after the August floods, it agreed a comprehensive package [13] of humanitarian and development assistance, civilian protection and reconstruction and economic recovery through EU trade instruments, in close coordination with other international actors (see page 95).

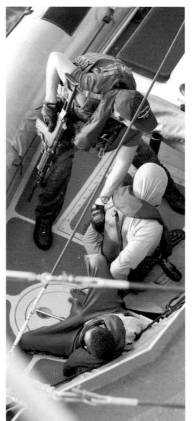

The fight against piracy off the coast of Somalia is an example of the EU combining its external relations instruments. The EU naval operation Atalanta [14] is complemented by efforts to boost the coastal states' capacity to try pirates. Maritime surveillance is being strengthened through reinforced partnership with regional states [15]. Aid to support Somali governance sits alongside funding for African peacekeepers in Somalia, and an EU mission is up and running in Uganda for training Somali security forces.

An EU commando boarding team on an anti-piracy mission off the coast of Somalia arrests suspected pirates.

EU SECURITY AND DEFENCE ACTIONS AROUND THE WORLD
Missions and operations in 2010 under the European security and defence policy

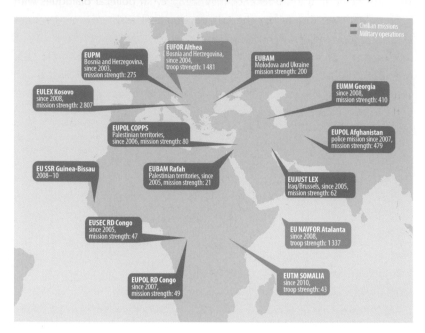

Source: Council of the European Union

To help Yemen tackle its multiple security, economic and political challenges, the EU developed an approach combining actions by the EU and its Member States with key international partners, in counterterrorism, humanitarian relief and support for economic and political reforms. The EU also established a full delegation there in January.

The EU was actively involved in reducing tensions and fostering the peace process in the Middle East. It vigorously supported the US-led efforts for successful negotiations via multilevel talks. It continued to offer political and financial support to Palestinian Prime Minister Fayyad's state building plan of August 2009. It insisted that for peace to be sustainable, a durable solution is needed for Gaza, that settlements are illegal under international law, and that there should be a complete stop to all violence. High Representative Catherine Ashton repeatedly visited Gaza on her trips to the Middle East. In Ramallah she met Prime Minister Fayyad, who also came to Brussels, where he appeared before the European Parliament and met President Barroso as well as speaking at the European Development Days in December.

Human rights are high on the agenda of all the EU's external relations contacts. This is reflected in the prominence they are given in political dialogues with non-EU countries, throughout the EU's development assistance programmes and in the EU's multilateral engagements. The EU's commitment to human rights has been further strengthened by the Treaty of Lisbon, which also paved the way for the EU to accede to the European Convention on Human Rights and consolidates human rights, democracy and the rule of law among key objectives of the EU's external policies.

Investing in peace

Through the EU's Instrument for Stability, conflict prevention interventions were launched in support of peace and reconciliation processes and stabilisation measures in Bangladesh, Belarus, Ecuador, Georgia, Honduras, Indonesia, Kyrgyzstan, Lebanon, Mauritania, Nagorno-Karabakh, the Philippines, Senegal, Sudan and Thailand. Altogether the EU launched 27 fast-track crisis response programmes in 2010, with commitments of €140 million — including €25 million for Haiti and €33 million in Pakistan. In addition, it mobilised €20 million to fund the EU Peacebuilding Partnership, which enhances the crisis preparedness capacities of civil society and regional and international partners, and another €62 million to address long-term security threats.

The promotion of democracy and respect for human rights were supported through election observation missions during the year, particularly in Africa, in Burundi, Côte d'Ivoire, Ethiopia, Guinea, Sudan, Tanzania and Togo. Under the authority of chief observers from the European Parliament, over 800 observers from all Member States staffed these missions, representing one of the most tangible and visible contributions to EU foreign policy, and bringing together Member States, Parliament and the Commission in a shared endeavour to promote democracy and human rights across the globe.

Advancing democratic elections

The executive and legislative elections in Sudan in April marked a crucial step in the comprehensive peace agreement which aims to bring decades of civil war to an end. The EU election observation mission comprised 147 accredited observers from 25 EU Member States. The mission's recommendations included the need for a comprehensive, transparent and accurate voter registration exercise and improved voter identification. The value of the mission is likely to be seen in the referendum planned for 2011.

EU observers check out a polling station during the presidential elections in Sudan — one of the many similar missions the EU conducted during the year.

Smaller election assessment teams were also sent to Iraq, and to Afghanistan, to witness the electoral process and to make recommendations. Although these operations are more limited, since they do not involve full observation, they demonstrated the merits of this approach in security-compromised contexts. Expert missions were also sent to Haiti, Kosovo (16), Nicaragua, Niger, Rwanda and the Solomon Islands.

EU efforts to promote the ratification and implementation of the International Criminal Court Rome Statute were particularly successful, with Bangladesh, Moldova, Seychelles and St Lucia completing the process during the year. The EU provided €4m to civil society organisations that raise awareness and promote ratification of the Rome Statute.

PARLIAMENT UPHOLDS FREEDOM OF THOUGHT

Cuban dissident Guillermo Fariñas was the winner of the 2010 Sakharov Prize for Freedom of Thought. The award recognised his non-violent opposition to and denunciation of the Castro regime, as a symbol of the struggle against the imprisonment of political opponents.

As part of its action to recognise human rights defenders and involve them in shaping EU human rights policy, EU missions were tasked with organising annual meetings with human rights defenders and their organisations, adopting local strategies and nominating EU liaison officers as contact points.

A toolkit (17) to promote and protect the enjoyment of all human rights by lesbian, gay, bisexual and transgender people was adopted (18). It prioritises decriminalisation, equality and non-discrimination, as well as support and protection for people defending these rights.

More than 40 dialogues and consultations specifically on human rights took place with countries across the world, including the first with Indonesia and Mexico. The achievements of the EU–China human rights dialogue and EU–Russia human rights consultations were reviewed. To maximise the involvement of civil society, seminars were organised in parallel with official human rights dialogues, including a civil society seminar on women's rights in June, where representatives from all central Asian states came to Brussels to discuss human rights issues as they affect women in the region. The annual EU–NGO Forum took place in July, where some 150 representatives of international human rights groups discussed the fight against the death penalty, protection of economic, social and cultural rights and EU relations with regional human rights organisations.

When the European Parliament awarded the 2010 Sakharov Prize to Cuban dissident Guillermo Fariñas, an empty chair dressed with a Cuban flag had to stand in for his presence. The Cuban government refused him permission to travel to receive the prize.

The Commission adopted a strategy for 2011–13 focused on strengthening the role of civil society in promoting human rights and democratic reform. It emphasises the fight against the death penalty, torture, children and armed conflict and violence against women and girls, as well as promoting the rights of the child.

TRADE — DOING BUSINESS AROUND THE WORLD

As the world's biggest trading bloc, the EU depends on and vigorously defends open trade. The World Trade Organisation (WTO) and the multilateral trading system are the focus for EU trade policy. The EU believes that a system of global rules is the best way to ensure that trade between countries is fair and that prosperity can be widely shared. The Commission set out a renewed, more assertive trade policy in November([19]). The new policy builds on a heavy agenda of multilateral and bilateral trade talks, but adapts the approach to better defend European interests, while also promoting European values and objectives. Trade is part of Europe's recovery plan and therefore an integral part of the Europe 2020 strategy. Indeed economic growth and recovery depend on open, integrated and fair markets. During the year, the EU created new opportunities abroad and ensured rules governing trade were strengthened and respected, making sure that trade takes place on fair terms.

The EU places a particular emphasis on developing new relationships with key trading partners, including the USA, China, Russia and Japan, where the biggest trade challenges are often about red tape beyond the borders, rather than the traditional lowering of tariffs at the frontier. To make life easier for honest traders while keeping security standards high, the EU improved its customs cooperation with strategic partners. With the United States, it sought mutual recognition of customs security standards — to avoid imposing excessive administrative burdens on legitimate business — and it opposed the imposition of scanning of all exports. The meeting of the Transatlantic Economic Council with the United States on 17 December took concrete steps to promote a forward-looking business environment that reduces regulatory barriers and encourages innovation, shared standards and high-tech business. Delegates agreed on a common approach regarding electronic health record systems, and to focus attention on access to raw materials, eco-friendly products, innovation policy, nanotechnologies, green procurement and social innovation. They also launched a joint website against counterfeiting.

EVOLUTION OF WORLD TRADE IN VOLUME
from Jan. 2007 to Sept. 2010, 2000 = 100 (CPB)

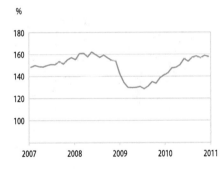

Source: CPB Netherlands Bureau for Economic Policy Analysis

The EU and Japan agreed on mutual recognition of customs security standards. With China, the EU has worked to strengthen customs enforcement of intellectual property right protection. And the EU–China high-level economic and trade dialogue took place on 21 December.

European Commission President José Manuel Barroso delivered a keynote address in Beijing in April. He stressed the shared interest of the EU and China in tackling global challenges such as the financial and economic crisis, climate change and energy.

Doing business with South Korea

The signature of the EU–South Korea free trade agreement, initialled in October 2009, took place at the EU–South Korea Summit in October, confirming the prospects for major trade developments. South Korea is already the EU's eighth largest trade partner, while the EU has become the second largest export destination for South Korea. The agreement provides for the progressive liberalisation of trade in goods and services, and for rules on competition and state aid, intellectual property and public procurement. To tackle non-tariff obstacles to trade, it includes specific provisions on electronics, motor vehicles and vehicle parts, pharmaceuticals, medical devices and chemicals. It will bring major benefits to economic operators and to consumers, as well as sending a strong message that trade liberalisation is a key element for the recovery of the world economy.

Negotiations for a bilateral free trade agreement were launched with Singapore in March, and with Malaysia at the EU–Asia Summit (ASEM) in October. An April summit with Japan agreed to mechanisms for strengthening economic and trade ties, setting up a high-level group to report back to next year's summit on ways of intensifying the relationship.

The EU and Russia concluded their bilateral talks on Russia's accession to the WTO in November. And progress in negotiations on free trade agreements with Canada and Ukraine held out the prospect of significant shifts in the global trade landscape and of new trade opportunities for EU businesses and investors in these growing markets. Significant progress was also made in the negotiations with India, with both sides agreeing on the broad contours of a final package at the EU–India Summit on 10 December. It was agreed that both sides would dedicate all efforts necessary to conclude the negotiations as rapidly as possible.

Flags from Vietnam, Australia and Thailand, among many others, flew outside the EU headquarters in Brussels in October when leaders from Asian and European countries gathered there to attend the ASEM Summit.

At the EU summit with Latin America and the Caribbean in May (see page 89), a new chapter was opened in trading relationships. This included a comprehensive region-to-region association agreement encompassing political dialogue, cooperation and trade, and a trade agreement with Colombia and Peru. EU and Mercosur leaders also agreed to relaunch negotiations on an EU–Mercosur association agreement covering political, cooperation and trade matters. At the same time, the EU's longest running trade dispute — on bananas, and the level of the EU tariff and preferences accorded to African, Caribbean and Pacific (ACP) countries — was solved in a way which is fair to producers in Latin America and in the ACP. A deal was signed with Latin American countries and with the United States. The European Parliament is set to ratify the deal in the first quarter of 2011.

The EU's longest running trade dispute on bananas was solved and a deal signed with Latin American countries and the United States.

The EU continued to address competition distortions in international trade via the use of its trade defence instruments (anti-dumping, anti-subsidies and safeguards), in full compliance with WTO rules. Sixteen new cases were opened and seven definitive measures imposed in the first 10 months of 2010. Despite the global economic downturn, trade defence measures in 2009 affected only around 0.5 % of trade. During the year the WTO issued its rulings on the dispute between the EU and the United States over subsidies to Airbus and Boeing. A WTO ruling in June criticised some of the low-interest government loans to Airbus. The EU appealed the ruling in July, while continuing to seek a negotiated settlement.

The Commission also made proposals in the area of foreign direct investment (a new area of EU competence following the entry into force of the Treaty of Lisbon), setting out how investment can be used to boost competitiveness and trade and lead to growth and jobs[20]. In October, to give a much needed boost to the recovery, the EU called on its major trading partners to remove more than 330 protectionist barriers and restrictive measures put in place during the economic crisis, and which, contrary to the G20 commitment reiterated at the G20 Summits in Toronto (June 2010) and Seoul (November 2010), have not been removed despite signs of economic recovery.

A deal was agreed on an anti-counterfeiting trade agreement, which helps to tighten up enforcement by developed countries, limiting the market for counterfeit goods and strengthening protection for copyright and trade-marked EU goods and products with EU geographical indications. Overall the EU continued to promote access to markets for EU goods and services through its local market access teams and, where necessary, through actions in the WTO.

Lifting restrictions on imports into Malaysia

Malaysia lifted cumbersome testing requirements on cheese from EU Member States in March. The measure, in force since 2008, implied that every consignment had to be accompanied by a health certificate and a certificate of analysis proving the absence of listeria in a probe of 25g. Malaysia claimed this to be an important and legitimate safeguard measure. The EU cited its own stringent rules and control measures and international standards development for listeria testing in 2009, and successfully argued that the Malaysian controls were disproportionate. The result not only promotes and simplifies trade — it also restores dynamism to EU trade which was already worth €3 million in 2008 alone.

Trade also plays a vital role in development and recovery. Better market access for Pakistani products was proposed by the Commission as part of the EU response to the floods that hit the country in August. The aim was to build confidence among investors and assist in restoring the economy. When approved, the proposed preferences would liberalise almost 30 % of Pakistan's exports to the EU — or €900 million of current trade.

WHERE DOES THE EU IMPORT FROM?
Share of imports into the EU,
Jan. to Oct. 2010

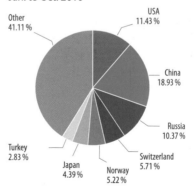

Other 41.11 %
USA 11.43 %
China 18.93 %
Russia 10.37 %
Switzerland 5.71 %
Norway 5.22 %
Japan 4.39 %
Turkey 2.83 %

Source: European Commission.

WHERE DOES THE EU EXPORT TO?
Share of exports from the EU,
Jan. to Oct. 2010

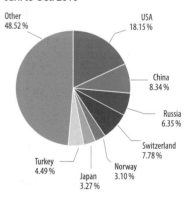

Other 48.52 %
USA 18.15 %
China 8.34 %
Russia 6.35 %
Switzerland 7.78 %
Norway 3.10 %
Japan 3.27 %
Turkey 4.49 %

Source: European Commission.

ENLARGEMENT

Accession negotiations with Croatia and Turkey continued in 2010, and new negotiations were opened with Iceland. The enlargement process has delivered benefits for Europe in the widest sense, including more security and prosperity for the Union as well as incentives for reform in countries seeking to become EU members. It also supported EU policies in energy, transport, environment, climate change and the security of citizens. At the same time, it consolidated contacts between people: notably, citizens of Albania and Bosnia and Herzegovina were granted visa-free travel to the EU as of 15 December, matching the facilitations from which citizens of the former Yugoslav Republic of Macedonia, Montenegro and Serbia benefited — also for the first time — throughout 2010.

CANDIDATE AND POTENTIAL CANDIDATE COUNTRIES

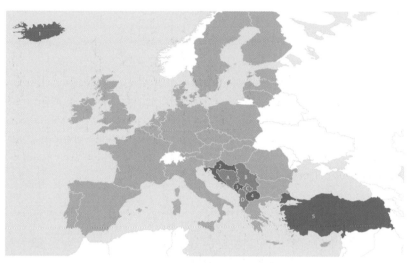

■ **Candidate countries:**
1. Iceland
2. Croatia
3. Montenegro
4. The former Yugoslav Republic of Macedonia
5. Turkey

■ **Potential candidate countries:**
A. Bosnia and Herzegovina
B. Serbia
C. Kosovo (*)
D. Albania

(*) Under UNSCR 1244/1999

Source: European Commission.

Reforms continued in all the enlargement countries, though at an uneven pace. These related to democracy and human rights, economic management and alignment of national legislation with EU standards and legislation. Challenges remained, notably in relation to good governance, rule of law and freedom of expression. Full cooperation with the International Criminal Tribunal for the former Yugoslavia (ICTY) remains a condition for the accession process for several countries, and bilateral issues also hampered progress.

Progress was made in regional cooperation in the Western Balkans and regional ownership strengthened. Work moved ahead on the Energy Community, the Central European Free Trade Agreement (CEFTA) and the South-east Europe Transport Observatory; the Regional School of Public Health Administration in Montenegro, financed by the EU, was opened. A revised memorandum of understanding was signed for regional cooperation against organised crime and serious crime in the Western Balkans. Regional cooperation was held back on some issues, however, by differences over the status of Kosovo. The European perspective for the Western Balkans was again clearly confirmed at the EU–Western Balkans high-level meeting in Sarajevo in June.

Among the **candidate countries**, **Croatia** further improved its ability to take on the obligations of membership, and preparations for meeting EU requirements progressed well. Thirty-four of the 35 accession negotiation chapters have been opened, and 28 are provisionally closed. Negotiations should be concluded once Croatia has met outstanding requirements in the fields of judiciary and fundamental rights, the fight against corruption, competition policy, public administration reform, support for minorities and refugee return. Croatia's relations with neighbouring countries, in particular with Serbia and Slovenia, have gained new impetus.

Turkey amended its constitution: reforms to its political and legal system address some priority actions in its judiciary and fundamental rights. But implementation of these decisions is needed, in particular to assure freedom of expression in practice. Accession negotiations advanced, albeit rather slowly. The current stage requires Turkey to step up its efforts, notably in complying with its obligation of full non-discriminatory implementation of the Additional Protocol to the Association Agreement. There was no progress towards normalisation of bilateral relations with the Republic of Cyprus. Turkey's more active foreign policy in its wider neighbourhood is an asset for the EU, provided it is developed as a complement to Turkey's accession process and in coordination with the EU.

In **the former Yugoslav Republic of Macedonia**, progress was uneven, with further efforts needed on independence of the judiciary, the fight against corruption, reform of public administration and freedom of expression in the media. Political dialogue also needs to be strengthened. In its November progress report, the Commission reiterated its recommendation on opening accession negotiations. A solution to the name issue remains essential.

ICELAND NEGOTIATES ACCESSION TO THE UNION

Based on a positive Commission opinion on **Iceland's** application for EU membership ([21]), in June the European Council decided to open accession negotiations; these were launched in July at a first Intergovernmental Conference. In November, the process of 'screening' the country's legislation for compatibility with the EU began.

© Norbert Eisele-Hein / Imagebroker / Belga

Iceland meets the political criteria for EU membership and, despite being hit hard by the banking crises, it is well prepared to undertake the measures needed to meet the requirements for EU membership.

Croatia achieved good overall progress in numerous fields and negotiations have entered their final phase.

Among the **potential candidate countries**, **Albania** established a constitutional and legislative framework, but shortcomings remain. These relate to: the effectiveness and stability of Albania's democratic institutions, notably parliament; continued politicisation of public administration; pending judiciary reform; enforcement of rule of law, notably in the fight against corruption and organised crime; and implementation of legislation on human rights. The Commission opinion, issued in November, on the country's membership application recommended that negotiations should be opened once the country has achieved the necessary degree of compliance with the membership criteria.

The October general elections in **Bosnia and Herzegovina** were generally in line with international standards, but the country must still amend its constitution to remove incompatibilities with the European Convention on Human Rights. Only limited progress in judiciary and public administration reform and in tackling corruption was achieved, but conditions for refugees and returnees and regional cooperation improved. Very little progress was made towards meeting the remaining requirements for the closure of the Office of the High Representative.

The interim agreement between **Serbia** and the EU entered into force on 1 February 2010, with the ratification process of the Stabilisation and Association Agreement starting in June. Serbia has continued to implement its reform agenda but additional efforts are required in the areas of rule of law and public administration reform. In October, the Council asked the Commission to prepare an opinion on the country's membership application. An EU–Serbia agreement on macro-financial assistance was signed in July 2010. Despite the cooperation with the ICTY, the two remaining fugitives — Ratko Mladić and Goran Hadžić — remained at large.

Kosovo made good progress on initiatives identified in the Commission's 2009 communication on Kosovo ([22]). Stabilisation and Association Process dialogue meetings were held, the first cross-border cooperation programmes for Kosovo were presented in December and expert missions assessed Kosovo's capacity in the areas of trade and reintegration. Important challenges remain, notably in public administration, the judiciary and the fight against organised crime and corruption. Following the advisory opinion from the International Court of Justice that Kosovo's unilateral declaration of independence did not violate international law or UN Security Council Resolution 1244/1999, the UN General Assembly adopted a resolution, co-sponsored by Serbia and the EU, welcoming the readiness of the EU to facilitate dialogue between Belgrade and Pristina. The mandate of the EU Rule of Law Mission in Kosovo (EULEX) was extended until June 2012.

MONTENEGRO: A NEW CANDIDATE FOR EU MEMBERSHIP

The December European Council endorsed the European Commission's November recommendation that **Montenegro** should be granted candidate status.

Accession negotiations will be opened once the country has achieved the necessary degree of compliance with the membership criteria. During the year, Montenegro made progress on the political criteria, the legal framework and administrative and institutional capacity. But increased awareness and sensitivity of the administration, police and the judiciary towards applying EU standards are needed. Also, the, rule of law, in particular in the fight against corruption and organised crime, remains a serious challenge.

EUROPEAN NEIGHBOURHOOD POLICY

Europe's foreign policy is both global and specifically local. Consequently, the EU has invested heavily, in 2010 as in previous years, in helping the countries in its own neighbourhood to resolve their problems and to become closer partners.

A report ([23]) on the countries to the immediate east and south showed how the European neighbourhood policy is promoting mutual understanding through its people-to-people contacts and through business, civil society and cultural ties. Despite a sometimes difficult context in these regions, the EU has been able to establish a partnership for reform with its neighbours since the launch of the policy in 2004. Tangible results have benefited both partner countries and the EU, even if implementation has sometimes lagged behind policy design and legislation.

INVESTING FOR THE FUTURE

By December 2010, just 30 months after its inception, the Neighbourhood Investment Facility had provided a total of €280 million in grants, mobilising a total of €12 billion in funds from European financial institutions. This money leveraged operations worth more than €7.3 billion, including investments in the field of renewable energies, such as a 200MW wind farm in the Gulf of El Zayt in Egypt and a wastewater treatment plant in Lebanon.

Particular progress was recorded with Morocco, including an EU–Morocco Summit in Granada in March — the first such summit with a Mediterranean country — and an agreement on the country's participation in selected EU programmes and agencies. Negotiations were completed for liberalisation of trade in agricultural products, and talks are under way on liberalisation of trade in services and investment. Tunisia, too, has discussed liberalisation of trade in services and investment, and has shown interest, along with Egypt and Jordan, in seeking advanced status in relations with the EU. Algeria agreed to set up a sub-committee on political dialogue, security and human rights. And a framework agreement under negotiation with Libya, where the EU decided to open an office, will pave the way for long-term cooperation and dialogue.

Association agreements are under negotiation with Armenia, Azerbaijan, Georgia, Moldova and Ukraine, with parallel negotiations for a trade agreement well advanced with Ukraine, and in a preparatory phase for others. Preparations were launched for new institution-building activities designed to help these countries in negotiating and implementing the agreements. New specialised sub-committees were created to strengthen EU bilateral relations with Armenia, Azerbaijan and Georgia. The dialogue with partners on human rights was also strengthened. Visa facilitation and readmission agreements were signed with Georgia, and preparations for negotiations of similar agreements for Armenia, Azerbaijan and Belarus were launched. Dialogues on visa liberalisation are ongoing with Moldova, Russia and Ukraine. A joint interim action plan was also agreed with Belarus.

Bilateral action plans with individual countries are complemented at regional level. The Eastern Partnership came into full operation, with two foreign ministers' meetings ([24]) which took stock of political achievements and reviewed the work programmes, in which more than 70 activities are planned. An environmental project for the region was launched in March to develop a shared environmental information system. With the Lisbon Treaty in force and the European External Action Service coming into existence, the new coherence of EU foreign policy-making now allows the discussion of issues of security and stability within the Eastern Partnership.

The regional approach in the south was pursued in the framework of the Union for the Mediterranean. Despite two postponements of the summit of the Union for the Mediterranean which had been due to take place first in June and then in November, sectoral ministerial meetings were held on water, tourism, trade, labour and employment, economic and financial affairs and the Facility for Euro-Mediterranean Investment and Partnership.

RESPONDING TO HUMANITARIAN CRISES

Together, the European Commission and the Member States constitute the largest humanitarian aid donor in the world. In the EU, humanitarian aid continues to enjoy strong support, as an EU-wide survey confirmed: eight out of 10 EU citizens think it is important that the EU funds humanitarian aid outside its borders [25]. The global humanitarian context is increasingly marked by serious natural disasters and diminishing humanitarian space in many crisis and conflict zones. Governments and non-state actors often disregard even the most basic protection afforded by international humanitarian law, further limiting the scope for humanitarian action. Meanwhile, the growing impact of climate change led to a sharp rise in the numbers of people affected by natural disasters in 2010.

Natural disasters presented huge challenges during the year. The Haiti earthquake provoked a swift reaction from the Commission's humanitarian and civil protection services. They sent experts to assess needs and coordinate the EU's response, mapped the damage and allocated €120 million in assistance. The Commission's Monitoring and Information Centre coordinated civil protection assistance from EU Member States, dispatching European rapid response modules and awarding €4.4 million in EU financial support for the transport of assistance. High Representative Catherine Ashton was able to represent the entire EU at the New York pledging conference in March. She made a collective pledge of more than €1 billion.

EU High Representative Catherine Ashton visiting a refugee camp in Haiti, March 2010.

© European Union

On 12 January 2010, Haiti was struck by the worst earthquake in its history. Over the year, the European Union provided both humanitarian assistance and development aid to help rebuild the country.

THE WORST FLOODS IN PAKISTAN'S HISTORY

The EU's humanitarian response to Pakistan's serious monsoon floods in August was significant. The Commission provided a total of €150 million in humanitarian assistance, and coordinated aid in kind from Member States, making use, for the first time, of civilian strategic airlift capacity in coordination with the EU military staff.

In sub-Saharan Africa, the EU also brought relief to victims of drought and floods, conflicts, epidemics and food insecurity. Sudan received €131 million to assist vulnerable populations in Darfur, South Sudan and the transitional areas. In the Sahel, funding eased drought and food insecurity. In the Horn of Africa, €20 million was provided to counter the effects of conflict and drought. In Kenya, the EU funded relief efforts in the Dadaab camps, the world's biggest refugee camps, and host to an increasing number of Somalis fleeing conflict and breakdown in law and order in their country.

The EU's civil protection mechanism was activated in response to six emergencies beyond the EU. Disaster risk reduction programmes were run in seven regions of the world. Every €1 spent on capacity-building, training and awareness-raising, early warning systems and contingency planning is worth €4 spent on humanitarian responses after a disaster has occurred. In October, the Commission proposed [26] improved efficiency, coherence and visibility of EU disaster response.

The EU provided relief to victims of 'forgotten crises', including the Lao Hmong minority in Thailand, the populations affected by internal conflicts in Colombia, Mindanao in the Philippines and the north of Yemen, the Sahrawi refugees in Algeria and the Bhutanese refugees in Nepal.

DEVELOPMENT COOPERATION

The Treaty of Lisbon recognises development as a policy in its own right, on an equal footing with other components of the EU's external policy. It puts a new focus on coordinating the Union's and Member States' development policies, and on coherence between development policy and the other EU policies. This coincides with a shift to integrate EU development policy into the Europe 2020 agenda. Moving away from a donor–recipient relationship, the policy is one of mutual interest: working in partnership with developing countries to provide sustainable and inclusive opportunities for growth and poverty reduction whilst at the same time benefiting the EU.

The money provided by the EU remains significant. Together with its Member States, the EU now provides nearly €50 billion of aid a year, a doubling over the past 10 years. As the world's biggest donor, the EU reconfirmed its commitment for its aid to reach the target of 0.7 % of gross national income by 2015. Member States, too, agreed to take realistic and verifiable actions for meeting their individual commitments.

The assistance provided by the EU is very tangible. The Commission provides over €600 million for food security per year, giving people both physical and economic access to the basic food they need. In the period 2004–10, 24 million people living in extreme poverty benefited from seeds and tools, direct cash transfers and food.

The €1 billion EU Food Facility agreed in 2009 is on track to providing a fast and efficient response in tackling food insecurity. More than 50 million people have benefited, and this is starting to show. Zimbabwe is a concrete example. There, 26 000 tonnes of seeds and fertiliser have been distributed to 176 000 vulnerable farmers. Geographical monitoring through satellite observation has also helped ensure effective implementation.

In March, the EU gave renewed impetus to food security in developing countries with two new policy frameworks. One focuses on progress towards the elimination of poverty and hunger, the other on maximising the effectiveness of humanitarian support in crises where food insecurity threatens lives. The Commission promoted the vision of an environmentally friendly and sustainable agricultural model, adapted to the reality of developing countries and markets. This enhances the productivity of smallholder farmers and the resilience of rural communities in making food available, accessible and of adequate nutritional quality.

SUSTAINABLE ACCESS TO SAFE WATER

Water and sanitation programmes, which help build infrastructure for drinking and wastewater systems, and provide basic sanitation and hygiene, amount to almost €400 million per year. Since 2004, more than 31 million people have been connected to drinking water and 9 million to sanitation facilities.

© European Union

The €1 billion EU Food Facility agreed in 2009 enables the EU to respond rapidly to problems caused by soaring food prices in developing countries.

Development policy underwent major evolutions during the year. With only five years remaining before the 2015 deadline for achieving the millennium development goals, the Commission delivered a series of proposals on development and education [27], gender [28], tax [29], financing, health [30], aid effectiveness [31] and food security [32]. Its approach to mobilising more financial resources for development was endorsed at the EU's June summit, boosting EU preparations in the run-up to the special UN review summit in New York in September.

DEVELOPMENT IS A GLOBAL CONCERN

At the G20 Summit in Seoul in November, the EU successfully argued for development to be included — for the first time — on the G20 agenda, firmly anchored in its growth and investment strategy.

Changes in global development architecture call for stronger coordination and increased synergies between all partners in favour of poverty eradication and sustainable development of the poor. The EU has accordingly strengthened development dialogues and practical cooperation with major strategic partners. Cooperation was relaunched with the USA with a focus on climate change and food security, and the first EU–Japan policy dialogue on development was held in Tokyo. Trilateral cooperation involving the EU, Brazil and Haiti has been agreed and practical preparations have started. A formal dialogue process among all those involved in development cooperation was started in March, to increase involvement of civil society and local authorities.

© Martine Perret / UN Photo

The EU has financed programmes to boost schooling — such as this project in East Timor, where younger schoolchildren receive mid-morning meals to encourage enrolment and attendance, and to increase students' learning capacity.

A 'Policy coherence for development' paper adopted in the spring outlined EU responses to the global challenges of trade and finance, climate change, global food security, migration and security. It proposed mechanisms to ensure that development objectives are taken into account and reconciled with other EU objectives [33]. The establishment of the European External Action Service is central in reinforcing this policy coherence.

An October communication on the future of EU–Africa relations[34] reflected Africa's role as a rapidly emerging economic, commercial and political actor. It identified a series of strategic areas where the EU and Africa could further enhance their relations for their mutual benefit, and suggested concrete steps for the coming years. The EU–Africa Summit — the 'G80' of today, with around 1.5 billion people represented at the summit table — took place in Sirte (Libya) in November, and set out an action plan for the two continents for the coming years under the heading 'Growth, jobs and investment'. The EU and Africa agreed to expand their bilateral cooperation in peace and security, democratic governance and human rights, energy, trade and infrastructure, migration, science and technology, ICT and space. They committed to working together more closely in international forums to make progress on challenges such as climate change and meeting the millennium development goals. Leaders also agreed to intensify the political and policy dialogue between both sides.

At the Joint ACP–EU Council in Ouagadougou in June, signatures were put to a revised Cotonou Agreement, on which negotiations were brought to a successful end in March. This agreement addresses the trend towards increased regional differentiation[35]. The new text reaffirms the commitment to attaining the millennium development goals, and strengthens the links between security and development. It recognises the role of the African Union, and confirms the commitment to political dialogue supporting multilateralism.

In September, the European Commission approved the first financing decisions under the €264 million 2010 allocation for the Vulnerability FLEX mechanism to help the most vulnerable African, Caribbean and Pacific countries cope with the impact of the global financial crisis and economic downturn. It helped 19 countries maintain their level of public spending in priority areas, and mitigate the social impact of the economic downturn. This short-term instrument, which provided €500 million during 2009–10, supported Antigua and Barbuda, Benin, Burkina Faso, Burundi, Cape Verde, the Central African Republic, the Democratic Republic of Congo, Grenada, Guinea-Bissau, Haiti, Lesotho, Liberia, Malawi, Samoa, Sierra Leone, Togo, Tonga, Tuvalu and Zimbabwe. This €500 million is in addition to the €1 billion Food Facility and the allocation of €200 million under the European Development Fund in 2008 to help developing countries cope with higher food prices. With these targeted mechanisms, the EU was the first to act in line with the recommendations from the G20 Summit in London in April 2009, working for a sustainable and balanced recovery.

Reflection took place on a new Council decision on relations with the overseas countries and territories with constitutional links to EU Member States, to enter into force in 2014. Its focus — modernisation, competitiveness and cooperation — was reflected in the annual political forum with these countries and territories, in March.

WHO GIVES DEVELOPMENT AID?
Main donors of official development aid. 2010 is a forecast.

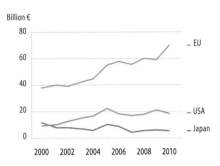

Billion €

Sources: European Commission, OECD/DAC.

PARTNERS IN CRISIS

Between 40 million and 80 million people in developing countries will be forced into absolute poverty because of the crisis. A set of measures was agreed with €215 million committed to help 11 African and two Caribbean countries to reduce funding shortfalls in their government budgets.

Trade is a major factor in the EU's relations with developing countries. The EU gives these countries unparalleled preferential access to its markets. This is done in part through the General System of Preferences, a trade arrangement allowing reduced tariffs for goods from 176 developing countries and territories. A public consultation during the year on future adaptations of this system was accompanied by a proposal to roll over the current scheme for up to two years to allow the European Parliament sufficient time to examine the new proposal to be tabled by the Commission early in 2011.

The development of economic partnership agreements is the cornerstone of the EU's trade and development partnership with ACP countries. Negotiations continued for all the African regions as well as the Pacific. They are most advanced with the Southern African Development Community. The Commission ensures proper implementation of those agreements which have already been finalised, for example in the Caribbean or Papua New Guinea. For interim agreements that have gone beyond initialling or signing, the process is to ensure consistency in different trade regimes, and to guarantee EU–ACP trade relations are on sound legal ground.

EU external assistance delivers results through cooperation with local communities and governments. The Commission strives to make the most efficient and effective use of taxpayers' money. But in changing times, it is necessary to ensure that development policy continues to be effective. Accordingly, a further consultation was launched in October on how EU development policy should adapt and evolve.

© Yves Horent / European Union

Sub-Saharan Africa continues to be the region in the world where the EU has its most important humanitarian projects. Here, a refugee camp in Burundi.

ENDNOTES

(¹) Council decision of 26 July 2010 concerning restrictive measures against Iran (2010/413/CFSP) (OJ L 195, 27.7.2010).

(²) Council decision establishing the organisation and functioning of the European External Action Service (2010/427/EU) (OJ L 201, 3.8.2010).

(³) EU–US Summit joint statement (http://www.consilium.europa.eu/uedocs/cms_data/docs/pressdata/EN/foraff/117897.pdf).

(⁴) http://europa.eu/rapid/pressReleasesAction.do?reference=IP/10/371

(⁵) Joint statement on the Partnership for Modernisation (http://www.consilium.europa.eu/uedocs/cms_Data/docs/pressdata/en/er/114747.pdf).

(⁶) EU–Canada Summit conclusions (http://www.consilium.europa.eu/uedocs/cms_data/docs/pressdata/en/er/114195.pdf).

(⁷) Joint statement following the EU–Japan Summit (http://www.consilium.europa.eu/uedocs/cms_Data/docs/pressdata/en/er/114063.pdf).

(⁸) Framework agreement between the European Union and its Member States and the Republic of Korea (http://www.eeas.europa.eu/korea_south/docs/framework_agreement_final_en.pdf).

(⁹) Fourth EU–Central America Summit joint communiqué (http://www.consilium.europa.eu/uedocs/cms_data/docs/pressdata/en/er/114558.pdf).

(¹⁰) Fourth EU–Brazil Summit joint statement (http://www.consilium.europa.eu/uedocs/cms_data/docs/pressdata/en/er/115812.pdf).

(¹¹) Joint executive plan of the strategic partnership (http://www.consilium.europa.eu/uedocs/cms_data/docs/pressdata/en/er/114467.pdf).

(¹²) http://europa.eu/rapid/pressReleasesAction.do?reference=IP/10/1282&format=HTML&aged=0&language=en

(¹³) Presidency conclusions of the European Council, 12 October 2010 (http://www.consilium.europa.eu/uedocs/cms_data/docs/pressdata/en/ec/116547.pdf).

(¹⁴) http://www.eunavfor.eu/

(¹⁵) Agreed at the Second Ministerial Conference on Piracy in Mauritius, 7 October 2010.

(¹⁶) Under UNSCR 1244/1999.

(¹⁷) Council note — Toolkit to promote and protect the enjoyment of all human rights by lesbian, gay, bisexual and transgender (LGBT) people, 17 June 2010 (http://www.consilium.europa.eu/uedocs/cmsUpload/st11179.en10.pdf).

(¹⁸) Adopted by the Council Working Group on Human Rights on 9 June 2010, and the Political and Security Committee on 18 June 2010.

(¹⁹) Commission communication — Trade, growth and world affairs: Trade policy as a core component of the EU's 2020 strategy (COM(2010) 612).

(²⁰) Commission communication — Towards a comprehensive European international investment policy (COM(2010) 343).

(²¹) Commission opinion on Iceland's application for membership of the European Union (COM(2010) 62).

(²²) Commission communication — Kosovo — Fulfilling its European Perspective (COM(2009) 534).

(²³) Commission communication — Taking stock of the European neighbourhood policy (COM(2010) 207).

(²⁴) In Sopot, Poland, and in Brussels.

(²⁵) Eurobarometer, August: '79 % think it is important that the EU funds humanitarian aid outside its borders.'

(²⁶) Commission communication — Towards a stronger European disaster response: The role of civil protection and humanitarian assistance (COM(2010) 600).

(²⁷) Commission staff working document — More and better education in developing countries (SEC(2010) 121).

(²⁸) Commission staff working document — EU plan of action on gender equality and women's empowerment in development 2010–15 (SEC(2010) 265).

(²⁹) Commission communication — Tax and development: Cooperating with developing countries on promoting good governance in tax matters (COM(2010) 163).

(³⁰) Commission communication — The EU role in global health (COM(2010) 128).

(³¹) Commission communication — A 12-point EU action plan in support of the millennium development goals (COM(2010) 159).

(³²) Commission communication — An EU policy framework to assist developing countries in addressing food security challenges (COM(2010) 127).

(³³) Commission staff working document — Policy coherence for development work programme 2010–13 (SEC(2010) 421).

(³⁴) Commission communication — The consolidation of EU–Africa relations — 1.5 billion people, 80 countries, two continents, one future (COM(2010) 634).

(³⁵) Council decision on the signing, on behalf of the European Union, of the agreement amending for the second time the Partnership Agreement between the members of the African, Caribbean and Pacific Group of States and the European Community and its Member States (2010/648/EU) (OJ L 287, 4.11.2010).

CHAPTER 5
MAKING THE EU MORE DEMOCRATIC,
EFFICIENT AND ACCOUNTABLE

The Treaty of Lisbon — in force since December 2009 — had an immediate impact on the work of the EU institutions in 2010. The focus of the Treaty of Lisbon is on delivering results to EU citizens through more streamlined and democratic decision-making. It reinforces the role of the European Parliament in shaping Europe. Parliament has new co-legislative responsibilities, which has enhanced its capacity to make decisions that have an impact on the daily lives, and to safeguard the rights of citizens. The Parliament has gained co-decision powers for 50 additional fields of legislation, giving it equal rights with the Council in agriculture, energy security, immigration, justice and home affairs, health and Structural Funds. For the EU budget, the treaty puts Parliament on an equal footing with the Council in deciding all EU expenditure and simplifies the decision-making procedure. At the same time, the treaty extended the use of qualified-majority voting in the Council to new areas, ensuring a more efficient decision-making process.

Better policy planning and improved screening of legislation is under way. Each institution has been fine-tuning the way legislation is prepared to maximise its efficiency and ensure the best use of resources. Numerous efforts to simplify EU rules and procedures are being undertaken to make their operation more transparent, to reduce unnecessary administrative burdens and to involve national parliaments and stakeholders more closely in the policy-making process.

New legislation is now routinely preceded by assessments of socioeconomic and fundamental rights impact as well as long-term viability. Existing legislation is checked for fitness of purpose. And legislation is introduced or modified to make many of the EU's own operations and those of its Member States more efficient — in everything from tax collection to transport. Progress has also been made with a view to enhancing transparency in fund management and working procedures.

IMPLEMENTATION OF THE LISBON TREATY

The EU governance has further evolved with the coming into force on 1 December 2009 of the Treaty of Lisbon. This has provided many opportunities for making the EU more efficient, democratic and accountable — ranging from a new degree of collaboration in economic governance to closer cooperation in tackling climate change, energy security, justice, immigration or organised crime. Many of these opportunities were rapidly taken advantage of during the year — as earlier chapters of this report have indicated.

Among the changes introduced by the Treaty of Lisbon, the European Parliament, the Council, and the European Commission have retuned the relations between themselves and with the Member States, so that full benefit can be derived from the new arrangements under the treaty. With a President of the European Council now in place, the role of the six-month rotating Council Presidency has been modified. This required a new form of cooperation from Spain, the holder of the rotating Presidency in the first half of the year, and from Belgium, which followed in the second semester, in the adjustments they made to their working methods to take account of the new arrangements. The Parliament exercised the powers it acquired — notably on international agreements — shaping, for instance, the final form of the deal that the Council had initially negotiated on transferring European financial data to the United States in the context of terrorist investigations.

President of the European Council, Herman Van Rompuy (right), and President of the European Commission, José Manuel Barroso, now routinely provide joint press conferences at the close of European Councils, as here in October.

The new President of the European Council, Herman Van Rompuy, played a key role in discussions on a new architecture for economic convergence and the Commission made use of its own authorities. For instance the Commission proposed mechanisms for strengthened coordination among Member States on economic governance, and it reinforced the links with national parliaments — to which the Treaty of Lisbon granted additional importance.

Arrangements for setting the EU budget have also been modified by the Lisbon Treaty. The Commission proposed the necessary changes to the financial regulation applicable to the Union's general budget and tabled a proposal for the multiannual financial framework regulation and for a new interinstitutional agreement on budgetary cooperation, transposing the provisions of the current interinstitutional agreement on budgetary discipline and sound financial management, in line with the Lisbon Treaty requirements.

The work in creating the European External Action Service (EEAS), which became fully active as of 2011 (see Chapter 4, 'The EU in the world'), also required a new financial regulation and staff rules [1], and new institutional mechanisms, since EU money that the EEAS spends must be subject to the same strict rules and wide-ranging controls that apply to all the institutions.

The Lisbon Treaty also modified the way the EU reaches decisions on many day-to-day issues, such as product authorisations or agricultural market regulations. The mechanisms have been clarified for delegating powers to the Commission to take these decisions, previously the 'comitology procedure'. In line with the treaty, a distinction has been made in the supervision mechanisms for quasi-legislative measures, which are referred to as 'delegated [2] acts', and straightforward implementing measures, or 'implementing [3] acts'. For delegated acts [4], the Commission is under the control (*ex post*) of the European Parliament and Council, while for implementing acts, the control is carried out by Member States [5].

THE EU INSTITUTIONS

The Parliament has exercised its new legislative powers, and had an enhanced say in other areas — notably on international negotiations, on the EU's future financing arrangements, and on the EEAS. The rotating Presidency of the Council has had to adapt so that it works constructively with a newly empowered Parliament and a President of the European Council, who has given renewed impetus to deal brokering. And at the current juncture of economic and financial turmoil the new Commission has continued to play an invaluable role in fleshing out proposals for exiting the economic crisis and promoting growth.

THE EUROPEAN PARLIAMENT

The European Parliament played its now-established role in the hearings for the Commissioners-designate of the Barroso II Commission in January — securing the replacement of one of the candidates: Bulgaria withdrew its initial candidate for Commissioner, and nominated another candidate. Following this, the Parliament endorsed the appointment of the new Commission on 9 February by 488 votes to 137, with 72 abstentions.

A resolution on the consequences for interinstitutional decision-making of the Lisbon Treaty was adopted in May. In the same month, Parliament opted for a pragmatic approach to its future composition to incorporate the additional 18 MEPs allowed for by the Lisbon Treaty [6]. The necessary minor change to the treaty was made in a short Intergovernmental Conference on 23 June. Member States are now ratifying this modification so that the new MEPs can take up their functions.

During 2010, Parliament took several measures to adapt to the Lisbon Treaty and to the evolving interinstitutional context. It updated the rules of procedure concerning parliamentary questions and delegated powers. Also, a new special committee ('SURE') was set up in July with a 12-month mandate, to help define Parliament's priorities for the post-2013 multiannual financial framework. The committee will report before the Commission makes its proposals in July 2011.

The Treaty of Lisbon has reinforced the role of the European Parliament (President Jerzy Buzek in the photo) through new co-legislative responsibilities.

© Petros Karadjias / AP / Reporters

The European Parliament also further developed its links with national parliaments, modifying its rules of procedure accordingly in June. Inter-parliamentary meetings throughout the year brought committees together with their counterparts from national parliaments to discuss the Lisbon Treaty's practical implications for EU policy.

In October, Parliament's President Buzek delivered a Presidency mid-term address, identifying eight priority areas where action is needed (financial crisis, solidarity, energy security and environmental protection, external action, human rights, women's rights, institutional reform and budget), stressing the need for innovative, non-traditional solutions to face the challenges of the future.

PROJECT EUROPE 2030

At the same time as the EU dealt with immediate concerns of democratic accountability and increased efficiency, it also recognised the importance of a longer-term perspective. In May, it took delivery of the González report 'Project Europe 2030', commissioned by the European Council in 2008 to provide a challenging vision of the next 20 years. Under the chairmanship of former Spanish Prime Minister Felipe González, a reflection group of senior European thinkers produced recommendations that ranged from education to energy, and from labour market reform to tax coordination. EU leaders at the June summit expressed their appreciation for the work, noting that it will 'provide useful input for the European Union's work in the future'.

THE EUROPEAN COUNCIL

On the initiative of its President Van Rompuy, the European Council met six times during the year. President Van Rompuy has started identifying concrete topics well in advance of the European Council meetings in order to allow for better preparation for discussions.

Immediately after the June EU summit, Herman Van Rompuy went to the European Parliament for a discussion with EP President Jerzy Buzek and the Conference of Presidents — in what was a first. He also debated the outcome of the European Council meeting with the whole Parliament at a special plenary session days later, in what has since become a regular post-summit feature.

THE COUNCIL

The rotating Presidency of the Council has had to adapt so that it works constructively with a newly empowered Parliament and a permanent President of the European Council. It was necessary for Spain and Belgium, the holders of the rotating Presidency, to establish their roles in a new institutional context, between the new players — the President of the European Council and the High Representative of the Union for Foreign Affairs and Security Policy — and the increase in the European Parliament's power as full European co-legislator.

© Christophe Karaba / Belga

In what is a first in interinstitutional cooperation, the President of the European Council, Herman Van Rompuy, regularly addresses the plenary session of the European Parliament after each European Council (here at Parliament's seat in Strasbourg).

Council configurations

The European Council modified the list of Council configurations to reflect the changes made by the Treaty of Lisbon, with a view to incorporating space policy in the 'Competitiveness (internal market, industry and research)' configuration and policy on sport in the 'Education, youth and culture' configuration. Consequently, the names of the Council configurations will from now on be as follows:

▸ General affairs;

▸ Foreign affairs;

▸ Economic and financial affairs (including the budget);

▸ Justice and home affairs (including civil protection);

▸ Employment, social policy, health and consumer affairs;

▸ Competitiveness (internal market, industry, research and space, including tourism);

▸ Transport, telecommunications and energy;

▸ Agriculture and fisheries;

▸ Environment;

▸ Education, youth, culture and sport (including audiovisual).

THE EUROPEAN COMMISSION

In 2010 the new Barroso II Commission formally took office following the hearings of the Members of the College by Parliament and its appointment by the Council. In the current context of economic and financial turmoil the Commission has continued to play an important role in fleshing out proposals for exiting the economic crisis and promoting growth. At the end of the year it adopted proposals which will serve to launch the debate on the future budget review, which will condition the way in which the Union revenue will be fixed. Likewise, the Commission has continued to improve the legislative framework by further working on the simplification of existing legislation and making significant progress in reducing administrative burdens and assisting Member States in the transposition of EU law.

© European Union

The European Commission 2010–14 at the European Parliament in Strasbourg.

The President and Members of the European Commission take an oath before the Court of Justice of the European Union on 3 May 2010.

In May 2010 all Members of the European Commission gave a solemn undertaking, before the Court of Justice of the European Union, to respect their obligations under the EU treaties. Being the first Commission that works under the new Treaty of Lisbon, the wording of the solemn undertaking was adapted to the new legal situation and included also a reference to the EU Charter of Fundamental Rights.

In 2010 the Commission again placed great importance on smooth and fruitful interinstitutional cooperation. Proof of which is the new framework agreement between the Parliament and the Commission (⁷) which updated and replaced the existing agreement from 2005. With the entry into force of the Lisbon Treaty, this new agreement is of particular importance, as it defines the relations between these two institutions after the European Parliament obtained strengthened powers, especially in the legislative process.

The new framework agreement between the Parliament and the Commission

The agreement sets out rules and a timetable for an intensified and structured dialogue between the institutions, which allows Parliament to give important input when the Commission is preparing its work programme as its contribution to Union programming.

Moreover, it confirms the Commission's intention to conduct a review of all pending proposals at the beginning of the mandate of a new Commission, so that they can be politically confirmed or withdrawn, taking due account of the opinions expressed by the European Parliament.

It sets detailed rules for how the Commission will inform Parliament about the negotiation and conclusion of international agreements and the possible inclusion of MEPs in the EU delegation as observers in international conferences.

It brings the rules for the protection of confidential and classified information in Parliament up to international standards, making it possible to inform Parliament on sensitive subjects — notably international negotiations.

It provides for enhancing the information provided to Parliament in relation to the work of national experts advising the Commission.

The agreement also reflects the 'special partnership' between the Parliament and the Commission that President Barroso proposed in late 2009. Even before the agreement was concluded, 2010 saw unprecedented cooperation between the two institutions — notably through structured dialogue between Commissioners and EP committees in the preparation of the Commission work programme for 2011, and through meetings between the College of Commissioners and the Parliament's Conference of Committee Chairs, and between President Barroso and the Conference of Presidents.

Earlier in the year, President Barroso presented the Commission 2010 work programme to the Parliament just six weeks after the new Commission took office [8]. This introduced innovations offering the right framework for the institutions to build a solid consensus on where Europe should focus its attention — including the first multiannual overview of possible future initiatives. In line with the principles of smart regulation, all proposals are then thoroughly assessed to determine which should go forward, and in what form. This is accompanied by a commitment to a constant review of plans year by year, a 'rolling' approach to enhance the transparency and quality of the Commission's work, while preserving flexibility to react to unforeseen developments.

During the year, President Barroso regularly took part in the 'question hours' introduced in 2009 in Parliament's plenary agenda.

In September 2010 he presented there the EU's first ever 'State of the Union' address [9], which he indicated would be a regular annual occasion to chart the EU's work for the following year and beyond. This listed the major upcoming challenges:

▸ dealing with the economic crisis and governance;

▸ restoring growth for jobs by accelerating the Europe 2020 reform agenda;

▸ building an area of freedom, justice and security;

▸ launching negotiations for a modern EU budget;

▸ ensuring that the EU exerts its influence to the full on the global stage.

The European Commission and the European Parliament have established a new partnership through the updated framework agreement. Here President Barroso addresses the plenary session of the European Parliament in Strasbourg.

These political priorities are reflected in the Commission's work programme for 2011 ([10]), which was presented to the plenary in November by President Barroso. He underlined its innovative institutional features and encouraged the Parliament and Council to engage in trilateral discussions on how to implement the treaty provisions on Union programming. The Commission invited the other institutions to give priority to urgent proposals in financial regulation and economic governance. The October European Council agreed on the proposal of the Commission to anticipate and 'fast-track' the proposals on enhanced economic governance.

To respond to the pressing demands in policy-making in energy security and climate change, President Barroso appointed a commissioner responsible for climate action — alongside commissioners for environment and for energy, and created two new directorates-general, one for energy and one for climate action. The previous combined portfolio for energy and transport was transformed into separate DGs and allocated to separate Commissioners. And to better respond to the challenges relating to citizens rights, justice and security a similar reorganisation was practised between Commissioners and DGs for justice on the one hand and for home affairs on the other.

THE NATIONAL PARLIAMENTS

Since the start of its term in 2004, the Barroso I Commission showed the great importance it placed on relations with national parliaments, by making the definition and implementation of a genuine 'national parliaments approach' one of its key priorities. In 2006 it set up a mechanism for political dialogue with the national parliaments, and began forwarding them new legislative proposals and consultation documents, as well as responding to parliamentary opinions. This resulted in around 500 opinions from the national parliaments during the Barroso I Commission, in addition to around 500 meetings between Commissioners and national parliaments.

The year 2010, however, was the first in which the Commission applied the new Lisbon Treaty provisions on national parliaments. The foundation laid by the Barroso I Commission meant that the positive evolution of this relationship and the smooth implementation of the subsidiarity control mechanism were notable successes.

The Barroso II Commission began work during a particularly important phase in its relations with national parliaments. The Lisbon Treaty provides for a significant increase of the role of national parliaments at EU level and contains a series of new rights and obligations, through which national parliaments are enabled to assume this new role. The new powers mainly concern:

▸ the 'subsidiarity control mechanism', also known as the 'yellow and orange card procedures'. This gives national parliaments the opportunity to force the Commission to review a legislative proposal (yellow card if objecting opinions reach a third of votes allocated to national parliaments) and also allows the legislator to stop the ordinary legislative procedure (orange card if objecting opinions reach a majority of votes allocated to national parliaments).

▸ the revision of the treaties (with, for example, a veto right for a single national parliament when it comes to invoking the bridging clause (or *passerelle*).

▸ the area of freedom, security and justice (right to information) ([11]).

The Commission conducted a stocktaking of opinions received from national parliaments in 2010, and of Commission replies or reactions, in the context both of political dialogue and subsidiarity control. In 2010 more than 80 Commission proposals had been sent to national parliaments under the subsidiarity control mechanism, and some 217 opinions referring to these documents were received, of which only 32 were negative.

A proposal that received particular attention from national parliaments, with eight negative, but also several positive opinions, was the seasonal workers directive ([12]). The thresholds for triggering the yellow or orange card procedure were, however, far from being reached.

Overall, the subsidiarity control mechanism is running smoothly. National parliaments' opinions continue to focus on the political content of Commission proposals rather than on subsidiarity issues. Since the treaty came into force, the Conference of Community and European Affairs Committees of Parliaments of the European Union (COSAC) has discontinued its organised subsidiarity checks on selected Commission proposals; its place has been taken by national parliaments, which are cooperating among themselves on an ad hoc basis.

Political dialogue between the Commission and national parliaments

The Commission's political dialogue with national parliaments allows a broader, more political exchange of views — not limited to legislative proposals and to subsidiarity. Under the political dialogue, the number of opinions received from national parliaments reached a total of almost 400 in 2010, thus increasing by over 55 % compared to the previous year. The advantages are multiple: the political dialogue improves the process of policy formulation and helps increase the Commission's own horizontal understanding of national dynamics and processes in that it brings the EU closer to the citizens. In addition, national parliaments can help the Commission to achieve objectives such as ensuring the proper transposition of EU law and a better implementation of EU initiatives.

THE COURT OF JUSTICE OF THE EUROPEAN UNION

The Court of Justice and the General Court made important rulings and took on board significant cases that have implications for a wide range of activities in the EU.

Some landmark rulings in different policy fields

- As to games of chance, the Court of Justice stated that a Member State can, under certain circumstances outlined in the judgment, prohibit the operation of games of chance on the Internet. This prohibition may, on account of the specific features associated with the provision of online games of chance, be regarded as justified by the objective of combating fraud and crime ([13]).

- The objective of combating the dangers of gambling has to be pursued in a consistent and systematic manner ([14]).

- The Court of Justice also ruled that legislation in France, Austria and Ireland fixing minimum retail prices for cigarettes infringes European Union law ([15]).

- In the field of sports, the Court of Justice stated that football clubs may seek compensation for the training of young players whom they have trained where those players wish to sign their first professional contract with a club in another Member State ([16]).

▶ In the trade field, the Court of Justice ruled that products originating in the Palestinian territories do not qualify for preferential customs treatment under the EC–Israel Agreement [17].

▶ The Court of Justice also explained the effect of the rules governing recognition by the Member States of judgments relating to insolvency proceedings, and notably specified that after main insolvency proceedings have been opened in a Member State, the competent authorities of another Member State are, in principle, required to recognise and enforce all the judgments concerning those proceedings [18].

▶ Furthermore, the Court of Justice was asked for the first time to interpret the scope of EU legislation on the protection of biotechnological inventions. It stated that a European patent can only be relied on in relation to an invention which actually performs the function for which it is patented and thus ruled that Monsanto cannot prohibit the marketing in the EU of soy meal containing, in a residual state, a DNA sequence patented by it [19].

▶ In the field of trademarks, the Court of Justice ruled that Google did not infringe trademark law by allowing advertisers to purchase keywords corresponding to their competitors' trademarks [20].

▶ The General Court delivered its first judgment on the Community design and annulled OHIM's decision to dismiss an application for a declaration of invalidity against PepsiCo's design for the shape of a 'rapper' [21].

▶ On access to documents of the Union institutions, the Court of Justice specified the conditions in which a request for access can be rejected, either for reasons related to protection of personal data [22] or to the protection of the integrity of the state aid investigations [23] and Court proceedings [24]. On publication of personal data, it clarified the conditions to be respected when adopting legislation imposing such publication [25].

The members of the Court of Justice in Luxembourg.

The new President of the European Economic and Social Committee, Staffan Nilsson, addresses a plenary session of the Committee in Brussels.

THE EUROPEAN ECONOMIC AND SOCIAL COMMITTEE

In the light of the Lisbon Treaty, the role of the European Economic and Social Committee (EESC) has also increased, through the inclusion of a horizontal clause on the social impact of European policies, new rules on services of general interest, and a stronger external role of the EU in general. A new Committee was appointed in October, and elected its new President, Staffan Nilsson of Sweden. Its work also focused on the economic and social crisis, on its Europe 2020 strategy observatory, on participatory democracy and on the European Integration Forum, co-organised with the European Commission.

The new President of the Committee of Regions, Mercedes Bresso, pictured during a meeting of the Extraordinary Bureau of the Committee in Antwerp.

THE COMMITTEE OF THE REGIONS

The Treaty of Lisbon enhanced the powers of the Committee of the Regions by giving it, for the first time, the powers to challenge at the Court of Justice of the European Union new EU laws it considers to be in breach of the subsidiarity principle. A new Committee was appointed in February, and elected its new President, Mercedes Bresso of Italy. During the year it organised events with Commission President Barroso and individual commissioners, and a start was made to revising the protocol of cooperation with the Commission.

The re-elected European Ombudsman, P. Nikiforos Diamandouros, gives a news conference to present his annual report 2009 at the European Parliament in Brussels.

© Olivier Hoslet / Belga

THE EUROPEAN OMBUDSMAN

The Parliament re-elected P. Nikiforos Diamandouros as European Ombudsman in January. Complaints he dealt with included access to documents, management of complaints concerning infringements of EU law, staff matters and issues relating to subsidies or service contracts. One special report concerning the Commission was sent to the European Parliament in 2010. The Commission adopted in June its annual evaluation report on relations with the Ombudsman and on the functioning of the internal procedure for replying to the European Ombudsman.

OTHER INSTITUTIONS

Other institutions also developed during the year. At the European Central Bank (ECB), a new Vice-President was appointed, and the Bank set up a Directorate-General for Financial Stability. It also made preparations for hosting the secretariat of the European Systemic Risk Board. Most important, the ECB contributed to the EU measures to stabilise the euro, notably with the securities market programme decided by the ECB's Governing Council on 10 May. Priorities in the European Court of Auditors' 2010 work programme included the multiannual nature of much EU expenditure, including flat-rate corrections and recoveries, innovation and the internal market, human capital, sustainable energy, and the Commission's strategy for simplifying the regulatory framework for business and citizens. It identified the advent of a new Parliament, a new treaty and a new Commission as bringing opportunities for improving the financial management of the EU, and it worked during the year to help the principal actors responsible for the management and supervision of EU funds to seize these opportunities for change.

AGENCIES

Four new agencies were created in the course of the year — the European Asylum Support Office, the European Banking Authority, the European Securities and Markets Authority and the European Insurance and Occupational Pensions Authority. The Interinstitutional Working Group on Regulatory Agencies, set up in 2009 with the aim to find common ground between the Parliament, the Council and the Commission on how to improve agencies' work, continued its activities in 2010. In May, it agreed a roadmap for the work ahead. In its November meeting, the group endorsed the work accomplished so far at technical level and had a first orientation debate on future work.

EFFICIENCY AND TRANSPARENCY

The EU has continued simplifying existing legislation and making proposals that reduce the administrative burden it imposes. Moreover, to ensure that new legislation and policies are of the highest standard, an impact assessment of all major initiatives is systematically carried out. Management and control of EU finances and transparency mechanisms have been further improved.

SMART REGULATION

The Commission's better regulation agenda has led to significant improvements in policy-making at EU and national level. The design of new legislation builds on views from stakeholders and evidence gathered through wide consultations and subjected to an impact assessment process that has been externally assessed as effectively raising the quality of proposals. In parallel, the Commission has carried out a thorough simplification of existing legislation and has made significant progress in reducing administrative burdens and assisting Member States in the transposition of EU law.

Ensuring a high-quality regulatory framework [26] for citizens and businesses is a shared responsibility for all EU institutions and the Member States. Such a framework is necessary for achieving the objectives of the Europe 2020 strategy for smart, sustainable and inclusive growth (see Chapter 1 for more details).

One of the Commission's duties is to ensure that policies at EU level are decided in a way that is evidence-based and proportionate, transparent and accountable. Besides, it has, through its 'Better regulation' agenda, made significant changes over the last five years:

▸ public consultations and impact assessment are now the norm for Commission initiatives;

▸ EU rules are being simplified;

▸ administrative burdens for businesses are being reduced.

Building on these achievements, the Commission has now taken a further step: a communication on smart regulation in the EU was adopted in October, setting out actions to further improve the quality and relevance of EU legislation [27]. In particular, the Commission will attach greater importance to the evaluation of existing legislation and policies. The resulting evidence will be put at the heart of the design of new or revised regulation when preparing impact assessments. At the same time, the Commission will continue to work with the European Parliament, the Council, the Member States and other stakeholders, and encourage them to pursue actively the 'Smart regulation' agenda. The voice of citizens and stakeholders will also be further strengthened by prolonging the consultation period from 8 to 12 weeks from 2012 onwards.

SIMPLIFYING VAT INVOICING

The Council adopted a directive aimed at simplifying VAT invoicing requirements, in particular as regards electronic invoicing [28]. Tax authorities must now accept e-invoices under the same conditions as paper invoices, and to remove legal obstacles to the transmission and storage of e-invoices.

ANTITRUST PROCEDURES MADE CLEARER

The European Commission has published a detailed account of how antitrust procedures work in practice in order to further enhance the transparency and the predictability of Commission proceedings.

LESS RED TAPE FOR SHORT-SEA SHIPPING

Administrative procedures were simplified for short-sea shipping, notably the new customs regulation and port formalities directive, in line with the action plan [29] on establishing a European maritime transport space without barriers. Further elements, including a single window for administrative procedures, the facilitation of third country calls and advanced electronic communication and information systems ('e-Maritime') are being pursued. This would offer potential savings of €75 million for the 1.7 million vessels that call at the main EU ports every year.

Simplification and administrative burden reduction

The EU is attached to simplifying existing legislation, and making proposals that reduce the administrative burden it imposes. During the year, the Commission made proposals that, if adopted by the Parliament and Council, could cut administrative costs by 31 % — way beyond the initially agreed 25 % target. The Commission work programme for 2010 renewed the multiannual simplification rolling programme with a list of 46 proposals for 2010–12, ranging across industrial policy, energy and transport, agriculture and fisheries, employment and social affairs, justice and home affairs, public health, taxation and statistics. The Commission work programme for 2011 updated the list of simplification initiatives and withdrawn proposals.

IMPROVED TECHNIQUES FOR TOURISM STATISTICS

Member States will be allowed to use estimation techniques instead of surveys for compiling tourism statistics.

EASIER ACCESS TO EU FUNDS

In May, a Commission review of rules for access to EU funds resulted in cuts in red tape and lower costs for beneficiaries, as well as more scope for combining public and private funding for a bigger investment impact.

IMPROVING CASH FLOW IN COMMERCIAL TRANSACTIONS

The directive on late payments in commercial transactions, approved in October, improves the cash flow of European business, and helps eliminate barriers to cross-border commercial transactions. It aims at establishing, as a general rule, a 30-day limit for payment of invoices in commercial transactions between undertakings.

The Commission continued to be supported by the High-Level Group of Independent Stakeholders on Administrative Burdens, chaired by Edmund Stoiber, the former Minister-President of Bavaria.

The Commission proposed a recast of the Brussels I regulation on jurisdiction and the recognition of enforcement of judgments in civil and commercial matters simplifying cross-border litigation and enhancing access to EU courts. The proposed new rules will minimise the length and costs of enforcing foreign judgments and ensure equal access to courts in the Member States.

In April, the Commission adopted a communication with options to simplify the management of research framework programmes, to make them more transparent and attractive to the best researchers in the world and to the most innovative companies, and in particular the smaller ones [30]. The Communication triggered an intensive debate with the Parliament and Council and with many other stakeholders. Consensus is building up on a number of short-term measures that can be implemented by the Commission under the current legal and regulatory framework, such as further developing the 'Research participant' portal, optimising the structure and timing of calls and better adapting the size of consortiums, introducing more flexibility for the use of average personnel costs or for the rules on interest on pre-financing.

Evaluation of existing legislation and impact assessment

At the same time, in 2010 the Commission started to systematically evaluate existing legislation *ex post*, indicating that all major existing policy instruments, whether expenditure programmes or regulatory measures should be evaluated on a regular basis. This is essential to ensure that regulatory measures form a coherent framework and deliver effectively on their objectives. It began reviewing the entire body of legislation in selected policy fields to identify potential overlaps, gaps, inconsistencies and obsolete measures, through 'fitness checks'. Pilot exercises started in 2010 in environment, transport, employment and social affairs, and industrial policy.

To ensure that new legislation and policies are of the highest standard, the Commission has also put in place a wide-ranging and ambitious impact assessment system of its major initiatives.

The purpose of this impact assessment system is to prepare evidence for political decision-making, and to ensure that all relevant policy options are considered. Impact assessment reports are published alongside major proposals to explain the justification and evidence-base behind them.

In September, a European Court of Auditors' report on the Commission's impact assessment system [31] confirmed that it is of real value to EU decision-makers, is effective in raising the quality of proposals, and represents international best practice in its transparency and its integrated approach.

The Commission will continue to strengthen the effectiveness of the system, encouraged by the Court's recommendations. An important step has already been taken with the publication on the Europa website of 'roadmaps' for all initiatives with significant impacts, outlining what analysis has already been made and what is planned. This has helped to improve the transparency of impact assessment work and facilitate the stakeholders' engagement at early stages of the policy preparation [32].

A key element of the system is the independent Impact Assessment Board, which continued to ensure that impact assessments conform to quality and procedure standards. It issued 83 opinions on the quality of Commission impact assessments and provided concrete recommendations for improvement. The board has been recognised by the European Court of Auditors as raising the quality of impact assessments. In 2010, some 66 impact assessments were carried out for major policy initiatives.

IMPROVING THE IMPLEMENTATION OF EU LEGISLATION

Work continued on improving the way that Member States apply EU law. In March, the Commission issued an evaluation report on the functioning of 'EU pilot'—the method introduced to improve responses to citizens and business on the application of EU law and to obtain earlier resolution of infringements of EU law. For instance, Commission services worked together with Germany to ensure that an important construction project did not have a negative impact on protected species in the area, and with the United Kingdom to ensure timely issue of residence documents for EU citizens and their family members. They also worked with Spanish authorities to protect consumers and the designation of origin of traditional products. In its report on these activities [33], the Commission highlights the full range of recent actions being taken to improve the application of EU law.

The Commission adopted a communication (34) on its policy to apply to the Court of Justice for the imposition of financial sanctions on Member States for the late transposition of EU directives under Article 260(3) of the Treaty on the Functioning of the European Union. In 2010 the number of infringement procedures initially launched against Member States for alleged breach in the implementation of EU law amounted to 1 168 (the figure represents the first stage of the procedure when a letter of formal notice is sent according to Article 258 TFEU). Those policy areas which saw the highest amount of inquiries being launched were health and consumer policy, environment, internal market and transport, representing over 70 % of the total.

PROTECTION OF THE EU'S FINANCIAL INTERESTS AND FIGHT AGAINST FRAUD

The Court of Auditors' independent assessment for 2009 showed a dramatic improvement in the management and control of EU financial management over previous years. This year, for the first time, the error rate for the budget as a whole was below 5 % — a success rate that few national governments could boast. For Structural Funds the error rate more than halved since 2008 and is now close to 5 %. And only 0.2 % of all errors detected imply suspected fraud. There is a huge difference between irregularities and fraud. Error rates do not mean that the amount is lost or wasted. Even when there are errors in financial procedures, the money may still have been spent in line with what was intended. For example, errors in a tendering procedure for a bridge construction project do not mean that the new bridge should be dismantled or that it is of poor quality. If errors with financial impact are discovered, undue payments are clawed back from the project or country at fault. The report notes that €1.22 billion related to irregularities were identified, reported and followed up, but the figure does not reflect the situation over a single year. These are irregularities reported by Member States in 2009, relating to irregularities which occurred over several years, and of this €1.22 billion, €1.09 million involved fraud.

The EU exercised more efficient control of EU money: €346.5 million of EU farm money unduly spent by Member States was claimed back in March as a result of a conformity clearance procedure decision adopted by the European Commission, and a further €265.02 million in July. The money had not been spent in compliance with EU rules, or had not been adequately controlled. The money returns to the EU budget.

In July, the Commission presented a reflection paper on the reform of the European Anti-Fraud Office (OLAF) at the European Parliament, as the basis of an interinstitutional dialogue between the Parliament, Council and Commission (35). The outcome of this dialogue fed into a proposal which the Commission will make in early 2011.

In March, a new system to report corruption and fraud anonymously via the Internet, the Fraud Notification System, made it easier and more secure for vigilant citizens and EU civil servants to report suspicious cases to OLAF.

There were also some intense debates over tax evasion during the year. Progress on increased tax cooperation was made in two areas: the Council reached agreement on strengthening mutual assistance between Member States in the recovery of taxes (the current recovery ratio is only 5 % of the amounts due) and in the assessment and collection of taxes (abolition of bank secrecy in relations between tax authorities, eliminating secrecy as grounds for refusal to meet an information request).

In accordance with the G20 guidelines on cooperation with offshore jurisdictions against tax evasion, the Commission proposed an amended anti-fraud agreement with Liechtenstein. This could also serve as a model for Monaco, Andorra and San Marino and, with respect to Switzerland, as a basis for a new or modified agreement, in particular as regards the exchange of information on tax matters in line with international standards.

Taking into account the VAT gap varying between €90 billion and €113 billion in the period 2000–06, the Commission launched on 1 December a Green Paper on the future of VAT so as to have a simpler, more robust and modern VAT system ([36]).

Finance ministers agreed in June to increase their cooperation against VAT fraud. They will do this by creating a permanent anti-fraud network, to be known as Eurofisc.

In April a new electronic system to monitor the movement of excise goods — alcohol, tobacco and energy products — gave the EU new capacities for combating fraud. It is estimated that about 100 000 traders dispatch around 4.5 million consignments of excise goods between Member States each year. The Excise Movement and Control System makes intra-Community trade in excise goods cheaper and simpler for operators, while also making it quicker and easier for Member States to tackle excise fraud. Member State authorities and economic operators can join the system progressively until 1 January 2011, after which it will be fully applied across Europe.

BETTER COMMUNICATING EUROPE

Three joint interinstitutional communication priorities for 2010 were: driving the economic recovery and mobilising new sources of growth; climate action and energy; and making the Treaty of Lisbon work for citizens. A first report was published, under the political declaration of 'Communicating Europe in partnership' 2008, on cooperation between the institutions and Member States in communicating on Europe.

A clear writing campaign, launched by the Commission in March, encourages the writing of shorter, clearer documents with less jargon, making them easier to read.

MORE TRANSPARENCY

A new framework governing the creation and functioning of Commission expert groups was adopted with the aim of simplifying and clarifying rules, and enhancing coordination. In addition, in order to improve transparency, a new version of the Register of Expert Groups was also set up, providing more accurate information on the type of entities listed, the groups' membership and activities carried out. And in May the Parliament and Commission relaunched work towards a common register and code of conduct for lobbyists. In October, an ex-Commissioner was required to resign from a UK investment bank's executive board after a European Commission ethics committee raised concerns over a possible conflict of interest — the first time the ethics committee had made such a ruling.

In 2010 the European Commission disclosed the identity of those who received EU funds in 2009 in policy areas including research, education and culture, energy, transport and external aid. The EU's online database of beneficiaries, now containing more than 114 000 entries going back to 2007, has been upgraded to allow more search options. In 2010, for the first time, the database provides information on Commission administrative expenditure linked to procurement contracts. Very few public administrations in the world have gone so far with financial transparency.

THE EU BUDGET 2011

In 2010 new procedures were applied for the first time for the adoption of the EU budget and proposals were also tabled to launch the debate on the future budget review, which will condition the way in which the Union revenue will be fixed.

The 2011 budget was approved on 15 December, the first budget under the new procedures in place under the Lisbon Treaty. The total budget for 2011 amounts to €141.9 billion in commitment appropriations, and €126.5 billion in payment appropriations. The Commission tabled a proposal for the revision of its financial regulation. Changes, subject to approval by the legislative authority, will simplify access to EU funds by cutting red tape and saving costs for EU beneficiaries, and extend the scope for combining public and private funding to get greater investment impact. Cuts in red tape notably concern waiving the obligation to pay interest on upfront payments, raising to €50 000 the current €25 000 ceiling under which grants can enjoy simpler administrative procedures, and making it easier for beneficiaries to pay project partners.

In October the Commission presented the budget review conclusions, with its proposals on both expenditure and new revenue sources for the EU budget post-2013. The main findings are that the current rules for the EU budget make it slow to react to unforeseen events while too many complexities hinder its efficiency and transparency. With public spending under pressure, it suggests ways to achieve a European budget that is up to the challenges, not necessarily through increased expenditure, but by focusing on the right priorities, added value, results and the quality of European spending. On the revenue side, it aims to promote a fair and transparent system that is understood by citizens and that reduces the EU's reliance on Member States' direct contributions by introducing new 'own resources'. Options include: a share of a financial tax; the auctioning of EU greenhouse gas emission allowances; an EU charge related to air transport; a separate EU VAT rate; an EU energy tax; and an EU corporate income tax. The Commission also proposed guaranteeing EU bonds issued by project promoters to fund big infrastructure projects.

THE EU BUDGET IN 2010

Sustainable development and innovation at the core of the EU budget

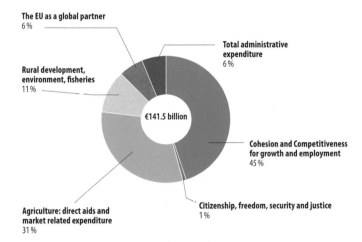

The EU as a global partner
6 %

Rural development, environment, fisheries
11 %

Total administrative expenditure
6 %

€141.5 billion

Cohesion and Competitiveness for growth and employment
45 %

Citizenship, freedom, security and justice
1 %

Agriculture: direct aids and market related expenditure
31 %

Source: European Commission.

WHERE DOES THE MONEY FOR THE EU BUDGET COME FROM?

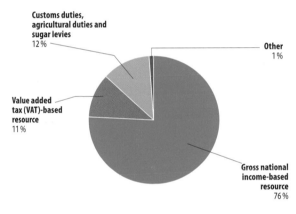

Customs duties, agricultural duties and sugar levies
12 %

Other
1 %

Value added tax (VAT)-based resource
11 %

Gross national income-based resource
76 %

Source: European Commission.

Parliamentary proceedings in 2010

Resolutions and decisions adopted by the European Parliament

	Legislation						Other procedures				
		Co-decision									
Consultation (¹)	First reading (²)	Second reading (³)	Third reading	Assent	Budget and discharge	Own initiative	Resolutions (Articles 103 and 108)	Human rights	Miscellaneous	Total
38	80	14		23	88	116	101	29	10	**499**

(¹) In 19 cases the European Parliament amended the Commission proposal.

(²) In 1 case the European Parliament rejected the Commission proposal and in 63 cases it amended the Commission proposal.

(³) In 7 cases the European Parliament amended the Council's common position.

ENDNOTES

(¹) Parliament and Council adopted in November the changes to the Staff Regulations and to the financial regulation relating to the EEAS, putting into place the conditions under which EU delegations in third countries can use EU funds — Regulations (EU, Euratom) No 1080/2010 and (EU, Euratom) No 1081/2010 of the European Parliament and of the Council (OJ L 311, 26.11.2010).

(²) Article 290 of the Treaty on the Functioning of the EU: 'A legislative act may delegate to the Commission the power to adopt non-legislative acts of general application to supplement or amend certain non-essential elements of the legislative act'.

(³) Article 291 of the Treaty on the Functioning of the EU:

'1. Member States shall adopt all measures of national law necessary to implement legally binding Union acts.

2. Where uniform conditions for implementing legally binding acts are needed, those acts shall confer implementing powers on the Commission, or, in duly justified specific cases and in the cases provided for in Articles 24 and 26 of the Treaty on European Union, on the Council.

3. For the purposes of paragraph 2, the European Parliament and the Council, acting by means of regulations in accordance with the ordinary legislative procedure, shall lay down in advance the rules and general principles concerning mechanisms for control by Member States of the Commission's exercise of implementing powers.'

(⁴) Communication from the Commission to the European Parliament and the Council — Implementation of Article 290 of the Treaty on the Functioning of the European Union (COM(2009) 673 final).

(⁵) Commission proposal for a regulation of the European Parliament and the Council laying down the rules and general principles concerning mechanisms for control by Member States of the Commission's exercise of implementing powers (COM(2010) 83). Parliament approved on 16 December.

(⁶) Article 14 TEU and Protocol No 36 on transitional provisions.

(⁷) OJ L 304, 20.11.2010.

(⁸) Commission communication — Commission work programme 2010 — Time to act (COM(2010) 135).

(⁹) http://europa.eu/rapid/pressReleasesAction.do?reference=SPEECH/10/411

(¹⁰) Commission communication — Commission work programme 2011 (COM(2010) 623).

(¹¹) Article 12 TEU and Article 70 TFEU and Protocol No 1 on the role of national parliaments in the European Union.

(¹²) Commission proposal for a directive on the conditions of entry and residence of third-country nationals for the purposes of seasonal employment (COM(2010) 379).

(¹³) Court of Justice rulings of 3.6.2010 in Case C-203/08 *Sporting Exchange* and in Case C-258/08 *Ladbrokes Betting & Gaming and Ladbrokes International*.

(¹⁴) Court of Justice rulings of 8.9.2010 in Case C-409/06 *Winner Wetten*, in Joined Cases C-316/07, C-358/07 to C-360/07, C-409/07 and C-410/07 *Stoß* and in Case C-46/08 *Carmen Media Group*.

(¹⁵) Court of Justice rulings of 4.3.2010 in Case C-197/08 *Commission v France*, in Case C-198/08 *Commission v Austria* and in Case C-221/08 *Commission v Ireland*.

(¹⁶) Court of Justice ruling of 16.3.2010 in Case C-325/08 *Olympique Lyonnais*.

(¹⁷) Court of Justice ruling of 25.2.2010 in Case C-386/08 *Brita*.

(¹⁸) Court of Justice ruling of 21.1.2010 in Case C-444/07 *MG Probud Gdynia*.

(¹⁹) Court of Justice ruling of 6.7.2010 in Case C-428/08 *Monsanto Technology*.

(²⁰) Court of Justice ruling of 23.3.2010 in Joined Cases C-236/08 to C-238/08 *Google France and Google*.

(²¹) General Court ruling of 18.3.2010 in Case T-9/07 *Grupo Promer Mon Graphic v OHIM*.

(²²) Court of Justice ruling of 29.6.2010 in Case C-28/08 P *Commission v Bavarian Lager*.

(²³) Court of Justice ruling of 29.6.2010 in Case C-139/07 P *Commission v Technische Glaswerke Ilmenau*.

(²⁴) Court of Justice ruling of 21.9.2010 in Joined Cases C-514/07 P, C-528/07 P and C-532/07 P *Sweden and Others v API and Commission*.

(²⁵) Court of Justice ruling of 9.11.2010 in Joined Cases C-92/09 and C-93/09 *Volker und Markus Schecke and Eifert*.

(²⁶) http://ec.europa.eu/governance/better_regulation/index_en.htm

(²⁷) Commission communication — Smart regulation in the European Union (COM(2010) 543).

(²⁸) Directive 2010/45/EU on the common system of value added tax as regards the rules on invoicing (OJ L 189, 22.7.2010).

(²⁹) Commission communication for the establishment of a European maritime transport space without barriers (COM(2009) 10 final).

(³⁰) Commission communication — Simplifying the implementation of the research framework programmes (COM(2010) 187).

(³¹) Special Report No 3/2010: Impact assessments in the EU institutions: do they support decision-making? (http://eca.europa.eu/portal/pls/portal/docs/1/5372733.PDF).

(³²) http://ec.europa.eu/governance/impact/planned_ia/planned_ia_en.htm

(³³) Annual report on monitoring the application of EU law (COM(2010) 538).

(³⁴) Commission communication — Implementation of Article 260(3) TFEU (SEC(2010) 1371 final).

(³⁵) Commission reflection paper on the reform of the European Anti-Fraud Office (OLAF) (SEC(2010) 859).

(³⁶) Commission Green Paper on the future of VAT (COM(2010) 695).

JANUARY

1
Spain takes over the rotating Presidency of the European Union.

12
Earthquake in Haiti.
Within hours of the disaster the EU provides aid for immediate relief activities and sends experts to the region. In total, the EU provided more than €300 million in humanitarian aid and pledged over €1.2 billion for Haiti's reconstruction and long-term development at the UN International Donors' Conference.

20
P. Nikiforos Diamandouros re-elected as European Ombudsman.

28
The EU announces new greenhouse gas emissions reduction targets for 2020.

FEBRUARY

3
The Commission endorses Greece's plan for cutting its budget deficit.

9
The Committee of the Regions takes up a new term of office.

The European Parliament approves the new European Commission 'Barroso II' by 488 votes to 137 with 72 abstentions.

16
The EU gives notice to Greece to remedy its excessive deficit by 2012 and recommends that the country bring its economic policies into line with the EU's broad economic policy guidelines.

MARCH

8
The EU agrees to grant around 45 000 micro-loans of up to €25 000 to the unemployed and small entrepreneurs.
The new European Microfinance Facility has a starting budget of €100 million, to be used over four years (2010–13).

15
The target of halting biodiversity loss and ecosystem degradation by 2020 is agreed by the Council.

25
Euro-area leaders agree to create a joint financial safety net with the IMF.
Under the agreement, Greece is to receive coordinated bilateral loans from other euro-area countries as well as funds from the IMF if in severe difficulty. The move is designed to restore confidence in the euro.

APRIL

14
An ash cloud over Europe caused by the eruption of a volcano in Iceland leads to the closure of much of European airspace until 21 April.
An estimated 100 000 flights are cancelled, leaving around 10 million passengers unable to travel. The Commission reminds travellers that EU passenger rights continue to apply, and sets up a group to help national governments coordinate. The crisis accelerates progress towards a 'single European sky'.

MAY

1
Opening of the World Expo 2010 in Shanghai.
President Barroso participates in the inauguration of the EU pavilion and leads a delegation of commissioners meeting with Chinese counterparts. The EU–China Science and Technology Week is held from 14 to 19 June.

2
Euro-area countries and the IMF offer Greece €110 billion in emergency loans over three years to help the country avoid defaulting on its debt.
In early 2010, rising government deficits and debt levels spark a crisis of confidence in European sovereign bonds and the euro. The market turmoil centres on Greece, whose 13.6 % budget deficit in 2009 was far higher than the country had forecast.

9
EU finance ministers agree on a €750 billion crisis fund to bolster financial markets.
Consisting mainly of loan guarantees from euro-area countries, the financial stabilisation mechanism includes a €250 billion contribution from the IMF.

12
The Commission proposes a package to strengthen the Stability and Growth Pact and extend surveillance.
The proposal sees national budget and policy planning being aligned through a 'European semester', allowing Member States to coordinate as they prepare their national budgets and reform programmes.

CHRONOLOGY

The events listed indicate some of the major events from 2010.
The chronology is not intended to be exhaustive — additional highlights
are detailed in the report itself.

OCTOBER

6
The Europe 2020 flagship initiative 'innovation union' is launched, aiming to speed up the development of new products and services.

8
A state of emergency is declared in three regions of Hungary after toxic sludge from an aluminium plant floods the area.

20
A new Presidency is elected for the 2010–13 mandate of the European Economic and Social Committee.

21
The European Parliament honours Guillermo Fariñas with the 2010 Sakharov Prize.

27
The Commission launches the Single Market Act and the Citizenship Report to enhance benefits of the internal market and remove obstacles preventing citizens and businesses from exercising their rights.

29
The Commission launches proposals for new industrial policy.

NOVEMBER

9
The Commission proposes an assertive trade policy agenda for the next five years to help revitalise the economy.

12
The G20 endorses the Basel III reform.
An EU initiative, this comprehensive set of measures aims at strengthening the regulation, supervision and risk management of the banking sector. It targets regulation, both at the level of individual banks and system-wide across the sector.

A new strategy is launched to secure a sustainable EU energy supply.
The Commission plans to propose legislation and other measures to cut consumption, create a single market by 2015, create a 'bloc' for bargaining with suppliers, and empower consumers.

17
The Council and Parliament agree on a framework for supervision of the financial system and establish the European Systemic Risk Board and three new supervisory authorities. The new system will be operational as from 1 January 2011.

23
The agenda for new skills and jobs is launched — a Europe 2020 flagship initiative to boost employment and upgrade skills.

28
The EU, ECB and IMF grant Ireland financial assistance of €85 billion.
The support comes in response to Ireland's request on 22 November. It is intended to safeguard financial stability in the euro area and the EU as a whole.

29
29 November to 10 December:
Cancún Conference on Climate Change.
Negotiations concluded with agreement on key issues, including forestry, technology transfer and a climate fund to support adaptation and mitigation efforts in the developing world.

DECEMBER

14
The Commission proposes enhanced cooperation for unitary patent protection in the EU. Patents valid in all participating countries can be obtained with a single application.

15
The European Parliament approves rules regulating credit rating agencies.
The European Securities and Markets Authority will directly supervise agencies. It will be able to make dawn raids, impose fines and ensure agencies evaluate the accuracy of their past ratings. It will come into force on approval by the Council.

The European citizens' initiative is adopted. For the first time people can directly suggest new EU legislation. If 1 million citizens from at least one quarter of Member States join forces, they may invite the European Commission to draw up legislative proposals in areas where the Commission has the power to do so.

16
Launch of the European Platform against Poverty and Social Exclusion — a Europe 2020 flagship initiative to ensure social and territorial cohesion.

17
The European Council agrees on an amendment to the treaty to establish a future permanent mechanism to safeguard the financial stability of the euro area as a whole.

18 The Greek government receives €14.5 billion from the EU, the first instalment of bilateral loans from 10 euro-area countries.

19 The Commission adopts a digital agenda for Europe — the first of seven flagship initiatives under the Europe 2020 strategy.

Severe floods in Poland.

JUNE

17 Iceland becomes an official candidate for EU membership.

The European Council gives the go-ahead to Estonia joining the euro area on 1 January 2011.

The EU adopts the 'Europe 2020' strategy, the new 10-year plan for spurring growth and creating jobs in the EU.

30 The Commission outlines a toolset to reinforce surveillance of fiscal policies, macroeconomic policies and structural reforms.
The 'European semester' includes sanctions to prevent or correct threats to the financial stability of the EU and the euro area.

JULY

1 Belgium takes over the rotating Presidency of the European Union.

New caps on mobile phone roaming charges come into effect.

A new logo for all organic EU products comes into force.

7 The European Parliament approves new capital requirements for banks.
The objective is curbing unsound remuneration practices in banks that have led in many cases to excessive risk-taking and contributed to the financial crisis. Banks must also hold more capital to cover their risks.

12 The Commission proposes changes to existing European rules to improve protection for bank account holders and retail investors.
Bank account holders, should their bank fail, would receive their money back faster (within seven days), increased coverage (up to €100 000) and better information on how and when they are protected. For investors, the Commission proposes faster compensation with higher compensation of up to €50 000.

26 The European External Action Service is established.

AUGUST

11 Pakistan hit by severe flooding.
The EU provides €150 million in humanitarian aid, while individual Member States provide an additional €170 million. Import duties on a number of export products from Pakistan are also suspended.

SEPTEMBER

11 Launch of 'Youth on the move', a Europe 2020 flagship initiative.
The initiative aims to increase student and trainee mobility and raise the quality and attractiveness of education and training in Europe.

21 Gender equality strategy adopted.

29 The Commission adopts legislative proposals to strengthen and expand tools for coordinating economic and fiscal policy.
The proposals also address macroeconomic policies and structural reforms. New enforcement mechanisms are foreseen for non-compliant Member States.

Getting in touch with the EU

ONLINE

Information in all the official languages of the European Union is available on the Europa website:
http://europa.eu

IN PERSON

All over Europe there are hundreds of local EU information centres.
You can find the address of the centre nearest you on the Europe Direct website:
http://europedirect.europa.eu

ON THE PHONE OR BY MAIL

Europe Direct is a service which answers your questions about the European Union. You can contact this service by freephone: **00 800 6 7 8 9 10 11** (certain mobile telephone operators do not allow access to 00 800 numbers or these calls may be billed), or by payphone from outside the EU: **+32 229-99696**, or by electronic mail via **http://europedirect.europa.eu**

READ ABOUT EUROPE

Publications about the EU are only a click away on the EU Bookshop website:
http://bookshop.europa.eu

You can also obtain information and booklets in English about the European Union from:

EUROPEAN COMMISSION REPRESENTATIONS

Representation in Ireland
18 Dawson Street, Dublin 2
IRELAND
Tel. +353 16341111
Internet: http://ec.europa.eu/ireland/
E-mail: eu-ie-info-request@ec.europa.eu

Representation in the United Kingdom
Europe House
32 Smith Square, London SW1P 3EU
UNITED KINGDOM
Tel. +44 2079731992
Internet: http://ec.europa.eu/uk

Representation in Wales
2 Caspian Point, Caspian Way, Cardiff
CF10 4QQ
UNITED KINGDOM
Tel. +44 2920895020
Internet: http://ec.europa.eu/uk

Representation in Scotland
9 Alva Street, Edinburgh EH2 4PH
UNITED KINGDOM
Tel. +44 1312252058
Internet: http://ec.europa.eu/uk

Representation in Northern Ireland
74–76 Dublin Road, Belfast BT2 7HP
UNITED KINGDOM
Tel. +44 2890240708
Internet: http://ec.europa.eu/uk

Delegations in the United States
2175 K Street, NW
Washington DC 20037
UNITED STATES OF AMERICA
Tel. +202 8629500
Internet: http://www.eurunion.org

222 East 41st Street, 20th floor
New York, NY 10017
UNITED STATES OF AMERICA
Tel. +212 3713804
Internet: http://www.eurunion.org

EUROPEAN PARLIAMENT OFFICES

Office in Ireland
European Union House
43 Molesworth Street, Dublin 2
IRELAND
Tel. +353 16057900
Internet: http://www.europarl.ie
E-mail: epdublin@europarl.europa.eu

United Kingdom Office
Europe House
32 Smith Square, London SW1P 3EU
UNITED KINGDOM
Tel. +44 2072274300
Internet: http://www.europarl.org.uk
E-mail: eplondon@europarl.europa.eu

Office in Scotland
The Tun, 4 Jackson's Entry
Holyrood Road, Edinburgh EH8 8PJ
UNITED KINGDOM
Tel. +44 1315577866
Internet: http://www.europarl.org.uk
E-mail: epedinburgh@europarl.europa.eu

There are European Commission and Parliament representations and offices in all the countries of the European Union. The European Union also has delegations in other parts of the world.